THE THINGS
OUR
FATHERS SAW

VOLUME III:
THE UNTOLD STORIES OF THE
WORLD WAR II GENERATION
FROM HOMETOWN, USA

WAR IN THE AIR:
COMBAT, CAPTIVITY, AND REUNION

MATTHEW A. ROZELL

WOODCHUCK HOLLOW PRESS

Hartford · New York

Information at woodchuckhollowpress@gmail.com.

Front Cover: B-17 Flying Fortresses from the 398th Bombardment Group fly a bombing run to Neumunster, Germany, on April 13, 1945. Credit: Public Domain, U.S. Air Force photograph.

Additional photographs and descriptions sourced at Wikimedia Commons within terms of use, unless otherwise noted.

Publisher's Cataloging-in-Publication Data

Names: Rozell, Matthew A., 1961- author.
Title: The things our fathers saw, war in the air : combat, captivity, and reunion : the untold stories of the World War II generation from hometown, USA / Matthew A. Rozell.
Other titles: War in the air.
Description: Hartford, NY : Woodchuck Hollow Press, 2017. | Series: The things our fathers saw, vol. 3.
Identifiers: LCCN 2017915746 | ISBN 978-0-9964800-7-9 (pbk.) | ISBN 978-1-948155-07-6 (hbk.) | ISBN 978-0-9964800-6-2 (ebook)
Subjects: LCSH: United States. Army Air Forces--Airmen--Biography. | World War, 1939-1945--Personal narratives, American. | World War, 1939-1945--Aerial operations, American. | Military history, Modern--20th century. | Air warfare--History--20th century. | BISAC: HISTORY / Military / Veterans. | HISTORY / Military / World War II. | HISTORY / Military / Aviation.
Classification: LCC D810.V42 R6911 2017 (print) | LCC D810.V42 (ebook) | DDC 940.54/8173--dc23.

matthewrozellbooks.com

THE THINGS OUR FATHERS SAW III

WAR IN THE AIR–BOOK TWO: COMBAT, CAPTIVITY, AND REUNION

For the mothers who saw their children off to war,
And for those who keep the memory alive.

How can I be a hero? I was lucky to get out.
— CHARLIE COREA, POW, STALAG 17

Dying for freedom isn't the worst that could happen.
Being forgotten is.
— SUSIE STEPHENS-HARVEY, REFLECTING ON HER BROTHER,
STEPHEN J. GEIST
MIA 9-26-1967

I think we shall never see the likes of it again.
— ANDY DOTY, B-29 TAIL GUNNER

THE THINGS OUR FATHERS SAW III

WAR IN THE AIR—BOOK TWO

THE STORYTELLERS (IN ORDER OF APPEARANCE):

CLARENCE DART

JOHN G. WEEKS

RICHARD J. FAULKNER

GEORGE T. FITZGIBBON

CHARLES P. COREA

EARL M. MORROW

SAM LISICA

JEROME SILVERMAN

THE THINGS OUR FATHERS SAW III

TABLE OF CONTENTS

AUTHOR'S NOTE   5

THE TUSKEGEE AIRMAN   19

'A TOUGH TIME'   21
REAL AIRPLANES   23
TUSKEGEE   27
TO NORTH AFRICA AND ITALY   32
COMBAT   33
LIFE BETWEEN MISSIONS   40
'YOU'LL GO WITH THE BOMBERS'   43
BERLIN   51

THE RECONNAISSANCE MAN   65

OVERSEAS   68
FLYING HIGH   71
THE LAST MISSION   75
WAR'S END   77

THE EVADEE   81

THE FARMER   84
THE FRENCH UNDERGROUND   85
LEAVING PARIS   86

THE P-38 PILOT   93

COMBAT   96
CAPTURED   99

MARCHED OUT   107
LIBERATION   109

THE FIRST ENGINEER   115

'COLORBLIND AS A BAT'   117
GOING OVERSEAS   120
THE FIFTH MISSION   121
'THEY JUST DEVASTATED US'   123
'THAT'S NOT HOLLAND, BUDDY'   126
THE OPERATION   128
STALAG 17   130
THE END OF THE WAR   133
'THAT'S HOW I FEEL ABOUT IT'   136

B-17 POW REUNION   141

TOGETHER AGAIN   142
MISSIONS   147
SHOT DOWN   151
ON THE GROUND   156
PRISONERS OF WAR   160
THE MARCH   170
LIBERATION   181
'THANK GOD EVERY DAY'   185

TRAILS IN THE SKY   191

ABOUT THIS BOOK   213

ACKNOWLEDGEMENTS   213

NOTES   217

Author's Note

The rooftop of a hundred-year-old valley farmhouse holds special delights as a midsummer's twilight approaches. I go out to sit back on the porch roof, watching the wind surf through the cornrows, the river flowing quietly in the background, maybe tapping my pack and lighting a cigarette before thinking about the day's events. Supper has ended, and the sun begins to quicken its march towards the horizon. And then I think I hear it. Far off in the background, a lone drone is steadily growing louder, creeping ever closer, steadier and steadier, like the slow but deliberate advancement of the shadows across the valley panorama. And suddenly she is here, almost treetop level overhead, her four engines roaring as she passes slowly, confidently, right over the top of me with a magnificence so bold I reach up as if to touch her underbelly overhead with my fingertips. An unrehearsed and authentic joy springs up from deep within me, for I have just witnessed something that future generations will never be able to even imagine: this lone sentinel gliding across the sky, the sudden manifestation of American air power and guardian of the memory of a past generation of Americans who once saved the world as the 'masters of the air.' My eyes locked upon her until she was nothing more than a speck in the sky.

I knew I would never forget that sound. Years later, three hundred miles away from the college town airfield in western New York where my rooftop reverie was broken, I heard it again from inside my classroom on a spring afternoon. I instantly knew just from that approaching low drone that it was my old Boeing B-17 Flying Fortress. I dropped the chalk and hurried away from the lesson, signaling to the kids to 'Follow me!' outside the schoolhouse doors. I'm sure they thought I was nuts, but I was just in time to look up and see that old girl once again disappearing over the treetops as she flew in for an exhibition at the local county airport.

I made my way out to the airport on Saturday morning to see my college town B-17. I had not seen her for years since returning back to the hometown that raised me, but I knew I would find a special person out on the tarmac—my old friend Earl. There he was, smiling, his cap embroidered with the emblem 'B-17 Pilot- WWII,' arms folded for the photographer.

Earl M. Morrow, 2000, Floyd Bennett Memorial Airport.
Credit: Rob Barendse for the Glens Falls Post-Star.

For years I had been collecting World War II narratives with my history students, and it had gotten newspaper attention. So he called me up and said, 'I just had to call you and ask—why are you doing this? Why are you interested in our stories?' Earl Morrow came into my classroom over the years, and I visited with him at his home in upstate New York, close by the communities that were dubbed 'Hometown, USA' during the war. He introduced me to his Army Air Force friends, and I had great conversations with them.

Earl held court on the tarmac that weekend, even going up again in the B-17 he once commanded over the skies in Europe, the aircraft he brought in 'on a wing and a prayer' over the White Cliffs of Dover, the plane that he and the survivors of his crew were forced to bail out of before she exploded in the leaden November skies over Nazi Germany. Little did he know he would soon share quarters with over 100,000 other prisoners of war of the Nazi regime, and then go on to reunite decades later with the men he was imprisoned with right back in this community not far from the waterfalls on the Hudson River in upstate New York.

*

In this and the upcoming books in *The Things Our Fathers Saw* series, we visit with more of the people who were forged and tempered in the tough times of the Great Depression and went on to 'do their bit' when even rougher times came calling. For those of you who may not be familiar with the background, most of these people either hailed from, later settled near, or otherwise have a connection to the 'Hometown, USA' community where I grew up and taught for over 30 years.

It's always been my philosophy that history is best understood when it is relayed by those who were actually there on the front lines. I was lucky enough to recognize this early in my career as a public high school history teacher, which began at a time when America was waking up and beginning to notice the deeds of the men and women who had saved the world only a generation before. Many of these men and women had never spoken of their experiences before, but on some instinctual level I sensed they were ready to talk, and more importantly, ready to share their experiences with our young people who were about to go out into the world themselves. So we began, slowly at first, to seek them out and invite them into the classroom. We taped our conversations and later wrote them out. I began to teach and write more intensely on the subject, and taught my students the value of communication with their elders. As time went on, my kids and I fanned out into our community on a greater scale; just 50 years before, at the height of World War II, it had been the subject of *LOOK Magazine's* multi-issue photographic profile of life on the home front, appropriately titled, 'Hometown, USA.'

After nearly three decades of teaching, I finally set out to keep the promise I had made to my students to write about the people that we had met and interviewed. My first book, *The Things Our Fathers Saw: The Untold Stories of the World War II Generation from Hometown, USA*-was well received and inspired me to continue with the series. In the second book in the series, we headed to the skies over Europe in *The Things Our Fathers Saw: War in the Air.* Several additional volumes are planned, including the war in North Africa and Italy, the D-Day invasion of Fortress Europe, and the piercing of the Third Reich itself to the end of the war in Europe. This book picks up where *The War in the Air* left off, with additional interviews about the air war over Europe that I could not include in that book.. So that it is not necessary to read the books in order, the background chapter on 'Air Power' from that book is re-presented in Chapter One.

*

As I also previously noted, as the writer/historian you spend days, if not weeks, with each individual in your book, researching their stories, getting under their skin. In composing their stories in their own words, you feel like you are giving them new life and placing readers at the kitchen table with that person who had something important to say. The reader shares the intimate moments with them as he/she gets absorbed in a real story being told. As an interviewer this happened many times to me directly with our World War II veterans, in living rooms, kitchens, and dining rooms all over 'Hometown USA,' in the classroom, and at reunion 'hospitality rooms' and hotel breakfast tables across America. As a history teacher I also turned loose a generation of young people to bond with their grandparents' generation in the same way. We gave all of our first-person interviews to research institutions so that they might not be lost. The New York State Military Museum was the primary beneficiary, with over a hundred interviews deposited for future generations to learn from. As one of the most active contributors to the program, I also leaned on them for video recordings of some of the interviews I edited for this book. My friends Wayne Clarke and Mike Russert, the workhorses of the NYS Veterans Oral History Program, traversed the state for several years gathering these stories under the leadership of Michael Aikey; they know the feeling of bonding with these extraordinary men and women well. In bringing these stories back to life, I hope I did a service to them as well as to the general public.

*

In the study of World War II, we are tempted to teach and learn the history as if the way things turned out was somehow preordained, as if it was a foregone conclusion that Americans and their allies were destined to win the war from the outset. As historian (and Pacific Marine veteran) William Manchester noted, because we know how events turned out, we tend to read the history with a sense of inevitability. Nothing could be further from the truth. It is easy to forget that during World War II the United States would be essentially engaging in two full-blown wars at the same time, taxing America's resources and families to the hilt.

Most of these men grew up very fast. Some left school in their early teens to work, some lied about their age to enlist or got a parent to sign off for them. Others found themselves commanding men at a tender age, where today they would not be afforded a legal drink. Listen to them tell you about the world they grew up in, how they surmounted challenges and obstacles placed on life's course, and how their generation of Americans not only rose to the challenge of defeating the greatest threat the world has ever seen, but also built the country and the freedoms that we enjoy today. Be inspired. Share their stories; give them voice. They have some lessons for us all, and we forget their stories at our peril.

Matthew Rozell
October 2017

CHAPTER ONE

Air Power

The transition of the young men in this book from the Great Depression to aerial combat, from boyhood to manhood, paralleled the American development of air power and the emergence of new tactics and philosophies of coordinating and waging 'air war' on a scale that had never been done before in history. The concept of waging war from the sky on a large scale after World War I was not a novel idea, but it was met with resistance by the established branches of the U.S. services. During the 1930s, proponents like Billy Mitchell, Jimmy Doolittle, and Charles Lindbergh made gains at home, as did the Royal Air Force in Britain. The German Air Force, or Luftwaffe, under Air Marshal Herman Goering, increased in size and range with the growth of Nazi militarism; these terrible weapons were tested during the Spanish Civil War and then the invasion of Poland to great effect. During the lull in the fighting between the fall of Poland in September 1939 and the German attacks in the west the following spring, Germany and Great Britain geared up for the battles that loomed on the horizon. The British had established the Royal Air Force, or RAF, as an independent wing of their armed forces. Led by independent thinkers who believed that air power and strategic bombing would be the key to winning the next conflict following its emergence in the First World War, RAF Bomber Command began their first missions with daylight attacks on German warships in the North Sea. In the course of a December 1939 daylight raid, half the bombers sent out as a force of 24 were shot down by the faster German fighter planes. The RAF quickly switched to experimenting with flying at night; survival rates for the planes dropping propaganda leaflets and the occasional bombloads thereafter improved dramatically, although bombing results were far less satisfactory.

After the German invasion of the Low Countries in the spring of 1940, British Prime Minister Winston Churchill issued a cautionary warning to the Luftwaffe that any attack on civilian populations would lead to an 'appropriate' response.[1] On May 14, the Germans bombed Rotterdam in the Netherlands, killing 800 civilians. Although part of the rationale for the Allied use of air power was precisely to avoid the constant slaughter that ground on and on along the stalemated Western Front for four long years in the First World War, no one could predict how much air power, once unleashed, would be difficult to contain. The first strategic targets were aircraft factories, synthetic oil plants, and marshalling yards for rail transport.[2] Wildly inaccurate, bombing by night led to much collateral damage.

After the fall of France in the summer of 1940, Britain stood alone. Hitler's plan, in simple terms, was to have the German Luftwaffe wreak havoc and terror from the skies, and have the U-boat fleet blockade the island country. Once Operation Sea Lion's first phase was completed, an invasion by navy barges and infantry troops could occur.

It never got that far. While London was initially avoided by German bombers, on August 24, 1940, two German pilots veering off course jettisoned their bombloads before heading home, hitting areas of the city. This gave Churchill the opportunity to order up an 81-plane retaliatory nighttime mission on the German capital. Though it did little damage, it was a public relations success, and

was also sure to bring German retaliation, which would in turn gar-
ner American public opinion towards helping Britain in some way.[3]
Outnumbered four to one, the pilots of the RAF, the use of newly
invented radar, and effective anti-aircraft flak kept the German
bombing campaign at bay.[4] In the ensuing Blitz of London, where
German bombers appeared over the city in a daily parade of terror
bombing, the RAF claimed 56 bombers over the city on a single day
in September.[1] Even the royal family's quarters were not spared, but
Londoners did not fold. Hitler called off the invasion indefinitely
two days later, though the onslaught would go on at night for the
next two months. Forty thousand had been killed in the Battle of
Britain, and the notion that 'civilian populations be spared' ren-
dered almost quaint. The strategic air offensive against Germany
would last for five years, 'the most continuous and grueling operation of war ever carried out.'[5] Hitler turned his attention to the East,
convinced that the conquest of the Soviet Union, with its teeming
agricultural lands and resources, was paramount to Germany's ulti-
mate victory in the war.[6] He could return to finish Britain off later.
And now, on December 6, 1941, with Hitler's legions literally at the
gates of Moscow, came Marshal Zhukov's massive Red Army coun-
terpunch. A world away, Japanese fliers were conducting last minute preparations for launching their strikes against a place most
Britishers, or Americans for that matter, had never heard about—
Pearl Harbor. Germany declared war on the United States on December 12, and the sleeping, lumbering giant stirred. The Americans would finally be on their way.

---

[1] *the RAF claimed 56 bombers*-The number of RAF kills on September 15,
1940, is frequently cited as 185, but both sides were obviously prone to ex-
aggeration; nevertheless, the punishment dealt the Luftwaffe that day
stunned the German High Command. See Dodds, Laurence, 'The Battle of
Britain, as it happened on September 15, 1940' *The Telegraph*, September
15, 2015.

*

In January 1943, Franklin Roosevelt and Winston Churchill met in Casablanca, French Morocco, to hammer out a rough blueprint for the Allied invasion of Europe. One of the first priorities was to destroy the German Luftwaffe, and as such, a 'Combined Bombing Offensive' was to be undertaken, with the Americans bombing German targets during the day and the British following at night in an unrelenting bid to soften German resistance. The goals were clear—in order to bring the war to an end, the effects had to be total and overwhelming. That meant bombing not only industrial targets but also densely populated urban centers where the working people lived; a skilled worker was more difficult to replace than a machine, and many machines escaped destruction in the bombing raids. Euphemistically termed 'de-housing,' British strategists in Bomber Command never denied that those efforts constituted an attempt to terrorize the population.[7] In Operation Gomorrah, the repeated attacks by the Royal Air Force and the Eighth Army Air Force targeting Hamburg during the last week of July 1943, more than 45,000 people were killed and 400,000 left homeless in conflagrations that resulted in manmade 'firestorms'—howling tornado-like updrafts which conducted superheated air skywards, drawing oxygen out of subterranean bomb shelters and incinerating human beings by literally sucking them into the flames.[8] In this one raid alone, more civilians died than in all of Germany's air attacks against English cities, though neither Bomber Command nor Churchill felt any moral qualms; many pointed out that the Germans had begun it with their raids over London during the summer nights of 1940. Given the brutal nature of initial German attacks and the necessity of defeating Hitler, this is hardly surprising.

'Typical bomb damage in the Eilbek district of Hamburg, 1944 or 1945.'
Royal Air Force Bomber Command, 1942-1945. 'These were among the
16,000 multistoried apartment buildings destroyed by the firestorm which
developed during the raid by Bomber Command on the night of 27/28 July
1943.' Source: RAF, Imperial War Museum, public domain.

More direct efforts to hit specific industrial targets fell primarily to the American air command. By the end of 1943 there were more than a million Yanks in Great Britain laying the groundwork for the destruction of Nazi Germany, with the American air bases dotting the eastern English countryside. From here, the Eighth Air Force mounted raids with her heavy bombers, the formidable B-17 Flying Fortress and the B-24 Liberator.

Boeing B-17G Flying Fortress "Shoo Shoo Baby" at the National Museum of the United States Air Force. Credit: USAF. Public domain.

The first mass-produced model, the B-17E, was heavily armed with nine .50 caliber machine guns mounted in Plexiglas 'blisters' and could carry a 4000 pound bomb load.[9] Subsequent models made various improvements, and from the beginning, the B-17 'Flying Fortress' was a workhorse of the American air campaign over the skies of Germany, with nearly 13,000 manufactured for the U.S. Army Air Corps. Improvements would gain the crews of the B-17 the capacity to carry three tons of bombs to the target, up to 2000 miles. The aircraft was also armed with thirteen .50 caliber guns.[10]

The B-24 Liberator was the most heavily produced bomber in history, with 19,000 manufactured; at one point, a mile-long assembly line at Ford Motor Company's Detroit plant cranked out a B-24 every 63 minutes.[11] It sported a twin tail and four engines, with a top speed of 303 miles per hour, ten .50 caliber machine guns, and the ability to carry 8,800 pounds of bombs. It was also used in a variety of capacities throughout the war. Complex tight bombing formations kept these bombers together to increase their accuracy and firepower against German fighters rising up to attack them, and several missions involved more than a thousand bombers carrying 10,000 or more airmen into enemy territory.

Consolidated B-24 Liberator from Maxwell Field,
Alabama, 1940s. Credit: USAF, public domain.

By the time the European bombing campaign ended in mid-April 1945, nearly 10,000 of these bombers would be lost, along with another 8,500 fighters and almost 80,000 American airmen.[2] Manning these planes and others, it would be up to the boys of the United States Army Air Forces to get the job done. They would come from the depths of the Great Depression, and they would become men.

---

[2] *nearly 10,000 of these bombers would be lost-*British losses were even higher, having been in the war longer. Miller, Donald L., *The Story of World War II.* New York: Simon & Schuster, 2001. 481.

Clarence W. Dart, Tuskegee Airman.
December 2003. Credit: Author.

CHAPTER TWO

The Tuskegee Airman

P-51 Mustang flown by the Red Tail Project. Credit: Max Haynes

The Tuskegee Airmen, or 'Red Tails,' as they came to be known, were a special group of airmen who trained at the airfield near the famed Tuskegee Institute in Alabama and would become the first African-American aviators in the United States military. Still segregated before 1940, the military had previously denied young black men the opportunity to fly for their country in combat. Historically, this was nothing new. The prevailing attitude that African-American recruits lacked the intellectual capacity and stamina for battlefield and leadership roles went back centuries; a mid-1920s military report reinforced age-old falsehoods and stereotypes about the combat readiness of the African-American soldier. Still, as war loomed on the horizon, the training of young black pilots, bombardiers, navigators, and supporting personnel began as a U.S. Army Air Corps 'experiment'—would these young people of color really be able to hold their own? Nearly a thousand men completed the Tuskegee advanced flight training program and went on to compile a distinguished record as the 332nd Fighter Group (eventually comprised of four fighter squadrons—the 99th, 100th, 301st, and 302nd) flying nearly 1,400 combat missions over war-torn Europe.[3,12]

Twice shot down by the enemy, Captain Clarence W. Dart managed to make it back to friendly lines safely, racking up 95 missions and receiving two Purple Hearts and the Distinguished Flying Cross with four oak leaf clusters, one of ninety-six fellow Tuskegee recipients of the DFC.[4] The Tuskegee Airmen were groundbreakers and paved the way for the ratcheting up of the civil rights movement and the eventual desegregation of the armed forces in 1948.

I interviewed Mr. Dart on several occasions. In December of 2003, he gave me and my class a wide-ranging interview that lasted several hours.

*

---

[3] The 447th Bomber Group was activated in January 1944, comprised of black aviators, several of whom were veterans of the 332nd who had completed their fighter tours and had rotated back home. They trained for the B-25 bombers, but the war ended before they saw combat; significantly, they distinguished themselves in standing up to overt racism at home. See 'The Tuskegee Airmen Story: The 447th Bombardment Group (M) (Colored)'; http://ecctai.org/tuskegee-477th-bombardment-group.

[4] *Distinguished Flying Cross with four oak leaf clusters-* the recipient has 'distinguished himself or herself in support of operations by heroism or extraordinary achievement while participating in an aerial flight, subsequent to November 11, 1918'-U.S. Department of Defense. Each oak leaf cluster represents an additional act subsequent to the first award.

'I live in Saratoga Springs [New York], a couple of blocks away from the racetrack.⁵ But no, to answer your question, I don't go there; in fact, I have never been there. Well, I could tell you why I've never been in there. When I first came back from overseas, they used to bring the horses in on Pullman cars all padded out with running water and everything, and compare that to what I saw in Italy, and in parts of this country, I said, 'They're treating those horses better than people,' and I said, 'They do not need my money.'⁶ So that's why I have not been to the racetrack.'

*

Clarence Dart, Tuskegee Airman

'A Tough Time'

The Great Depression was a tough time. To think of the way people had to live. People who had good jobs and lost them overnight because of the Crash in 1929, when the stock market crashed on Wall Street. Overnight, millionaires became paupers. No money, period. A lot of people, believe it or not, jumped out of those windows down there in New York City and committed suicide; the shock was just that great. To think that they were penniless overnight because they bought stocks on what they call 'margins.' It wasn't enough to cover or reserve when the market collapsed, and so they just became penniless overnight.

---

⁵ *the racetrack*- Saratoga Race Course is one of the nation's oldest thoroughbred horse racing tracks, opening in the summer of 1863.

⁶ *Pullman cars all padded out with running water*- specially-padded railroad boxcars were equipped with feeding and watering apparatus specifically for transporting racehorses; the purpose was to reduce the stress and fatigue of travel for the horse, which sometimes had to compete shortly after arrival.

It affected everybody. People were selling apples for a nickel on street corners. My father, fortunately, didn't lose his job because he worked on the railroad, but he kept taking pay cuts all the way through the Depression until the time it started to turn around when World War II started; I think he was down under twenty-five dollars a week, take-home pay. We had just bought a house, and boy, did we struggle during that time! I could take the whole afternoon telling you how we lived and what my mother used to do to keep me in clothes. My mother would buy shirts from the Salvation Army store. She would turn the collars because they would get frayed. She would take the collars off, turn them, and sew them back onto the shirts. It was a time when people really had to be on their own.

I could remember, especially in the winter, we had what you called garters, but they were rubber boots, no insulation in the darn things. We would go out and play until we couldn't feel anything in our feet and hands. You would come home and the first thing, [your parents would] put you in tepid water, supposedly to warm you up. As soon as you hit that water, you would start screaming. I don't know if any of you have had frostbite or anything like that, from being out skiing or ice skating until your hands get so cold you don't feel anything anymore. It lasts practically forever. Once it happens to you, you will always feel that cold. I experienced it again, so to speak, when we were flying—switched to the P-51s, at high altitudes, around anywhere from twenty-five thousand to over thirty thousand feet. There wasn't much heat in the airplanes. The heat in the P-51s would come in on one side and that foot would get warm, but you would have to sort of cross your feet [laughs] to defrost the other foot. I'll get to that further on to make a continuity.

Of course, it also brought people together. There was some welfare help, but it was tough, especially in the wintertime. We kids used to go down and stand next to the railroad tracks. The firemen on the locomotives used to shovel coal off of the engines as they went by. We would pick up the coal and take it home. Of course, we burned everything; we didn't have central heating in homes in those days. Everybody had either a fireplace or a big central furnace with one duct on the top that supposedly was to heat the whole house. We used to go out and pick wild mustards and stuff like that for food. Everyone had a garden also. There was a lot of implementation to survive.

Real Airplanes

When the war started in 1941, I had just turned twenty-one. I was singing in our church choir at our radio station that afternoon when they came in and said that Pearl Harbor had been bombed. I had just turned 21 on December 6, and it happened the next day. A friend and I were talking about going into the Navy. But my mother put a stop to that right quick. She said, 'You're not going into any army, navy, or anything.' Well, you know how mothers are; they're still that way today.

As a kid I always built model airplanes because I was an airplane fanatic. It was after I saw the first airplane fly, then they started selling these kits. First, it was mostly these little gliders you can throw around. Then I graduated to building replicas of real airplanes. There were a lot at fairs then, not like nowadays. I can remember being angry with my mother because when I was a kid they used to have these hobby shows; kids would get prizes by being judged on their workmanship. I had built this model of a Curtiss Goshawk, a Navy fighter. There were a few mistakes in the thing, so I didn't want it exhibited, but my mother, she was so proud of it [laughs] she took it to the show and put it in there. I didn't win anything, but she was proud enough that she wanted it exhibited. Anyway, I was always fascinated with flying.

When the war started, and after a lot of pressure started from politicians, Mrs. Roosevelt and other people decided they would train black pilots. I have commentary on this because in spite of what black soldiers and sailors have done in the history of this country, it was always convenient just to forget what they did, from the Revolution right on up until this day. They fight in Albany about getting the Congressional Medal of Honor for Henry Johnson.[7] It shouldn't have happened. He did as much as what's-his-name [Sergeant York] did in World War I. I guess he killed about ten German soldiers that had attacked his group. At the end he was fighting with a knife. He used up all of his ammunition and saved a lot of his squad.

But when they decided to train black pilots, the assessment team came through, well, let me back up...

After high school, there were no jobs, so I went to what they called Elmira Aviation Ground School. The state figured they would start all these training schools for people to learn how to be mechanics, machinists, and radio operators. I took all the classes that I could. I figured I was set to do anything, but you go around, and how things were in those days, you were rejected for one reason or another. When the assessment team from the Air Corps came around with their tests, I passed all their tests, except my medical. Most of my medical was all right, except I didn't pass the depth perception test. That was because I was so excited I didn't get sleep the night before! My eyesight was kind of fuzzy. In those days, the depth perception test used two sticks. One of the sticks had a line

---

[7] *Medal of Honor for Henry Johnson*-Johnson, a New Yorker, fought with the 'Harlem Hellcats' on the front lines in France, the first American to receive the Croix de Guerre, France's highest award for bravery. At the time of our 2003 interview with Mr. Dart, a renewed effort to have Johnson formally awarded the medal had just been blocked. On June 2, 2015, President Obama presented the MOH to the head of the NYS National Guard, as Johnson had died in obscurity in 1929.

on it, and you had to move the sticks until they were opposite each other. This was supposed to demonstrate your depth perception so when you came in to land [*laughs*], you knew how far the ground was below you or something like that. But it was a rudimentary test. Anyway, they told me, 'You go back and get rested. So when we come back again we'll give you another test.' That happened about eight months after that. So I came around and passed the test. They said, 'Go home. When your class is called, we'll cut orders and give you the oath of office. We will see you get to Tuskegee for training.' Well, they were still building the field down there in Tuskegee, so I didn't feel too bad about it. I told my draft board that I was going into the Air Corps.

I guess they didn't believe me because I was around for almost six months, and next thing I knew, I got my 'Greetings from Uncle Sam.' Have any of you heard your father or grandfather talk about greetings from Uncle Sam? Well, that's what the letter said: 'Greetings.' [*Laughs*] Next thing I knew, I was on a train to Fort Niagara, which was the classification center for our part of the state where they decided where you were going to go. The first thing they told us was, 'Well, we don't know what you can do, just tell us what you would like to do,' and so on and so forth. I put down all the things I had learned: airplane mechanics, machinist, and radio operator.

I didn't get to go anyplace I asked. Next thing I knew, I was on a train to Fort Sill, Oklahoma, for field artillery. I said, 'Oh my goodness, I'm not going to learn how to fly.' But then, I committed a cardinal sin in the military. I didn't go through channels! See, in the military, if you're one of the lower ranks and you want to do something, you go to your squad commander, and he passes it on to the company commander, and if the company commander sees fit, he will forward it. I wrote this letter to the commanding general of the Air Corps! That's against the law [*laughs*]. I bypassed everybody, and in headquarters I think they realized I made a mistake. They wrote my father but not me. He told me that they had said not to worry, because they knew where I was. When the field school was finished and my class was called, they would cut orders and have me sent to Tuskegee.

Well, meanwhile, I didn't mind the field artillery because it was fun shooting those big guns, 155mm howitzers. I think I shot every gun type that the military had at the time, at least the ground troops—all kinds of machine guns. They had pistols from the cavalry, the kind that you see, those long-barreled pistols, in the movies. We had those kinds of pistols, and shotguns, and tank weapons. When my orders came through, they came through on a Friday evening; no, I think they came during the day. But my company commander didn't tell me until after retreat on that Friday. I think he was kind of angry with me because I had taken a lot of math in high school; I used to aim in my section, my howitzer section. To aim those big guns, they have what they call an aiming stick, which is behind the gun. There was a periscope-type thing on the breech of the gun. You look through that periscope back at the aiming stick to traverse the gun. They called down the elevation that they wanted you to fire the gun at. I was made chief of section because I had pretty a good math background and didn't have any trouble with triangulating a gun.

I turned him down on [becoming second lieutenant] because through the 'scuttlebutt' I had heard what had happened to second lieutenants in the field artillery—they made them forward observers! They sent them to places, especially over the Pacific. The Japanese would figure out who was calling down fire on them. They search out the forward observers, and, naturally, they didn't last long. So we knew all this stuff and I turned him down. And he was disappointed because he thought I would jump at the chance to become an officer and second lieutenant. I told him, 'No, I am going into the Air Corps.' Well, he didn't believe me, but I did get my orders. He waited until after retreat on a Friday, and I had to go to Oklahoma City to catch a train to go to Tuskegee.

Tuskegee

I had a lot of friends. They said, 'Oh, we will help you out.' They went up to the office and forged signatures and got me transportation to get to Oklahoma City to catch a train to Tuskegee. They of course could have gotten court marshaled for it. [*Laughs*] I arrived at a little town called Cheaha at about two o'clock in the morning— it was way out in the boonies. There was a telephone pole with one little light that looked like a sixty watt bulb. [*Laughs*] It was raining and not really a train station, but out in the boonies. Pretty soon there came about three 6x6 trucks. They put us in the trucks and took us out to the field.

Before I left Fort Sill I tried to give my overcoat back. I told the quartermaster, or the guy that worked in the quartermaster's section, that I didn't need it anymore because I was going to southern Alabama where it was nice and warm. He made me keep my overcoat. When we got to the field there was nobody who had been designated to start a fire in the furnace in the barracks. They were brand-new barracks. So we had to sleep in our clothes the first night. The next morning when we woke up they had these big water barrels at the corner of each barrack. There was ice about an inch thick on the water of those barrels. I guess they were supposed to be in case of a fire, to help put a fire out. I learned about the South that it can get just as cold down there as it does up in the north! I was glad I had that coat.

Eventually, they got us settled down. Some of us were transferred to the campus of the Tuskegee Institute for our ground training, to learn navigation and communications and stuff like that. I didn't have any trouble because I had had the experience of radio and so forth. Eventually, while we were there, after we passed our tests in ground school, they would truck us each day out to Moton Field, the field which I told you is going to be a national [park] monument. We trained in PT-17s, which were biplanes built by Stearman Company.[8] It was the thrill of my life!

PT-17 trainer. 'Spirit of Tuskegee.' Credit: Rennett Stowe

When I was going to the ground school, I used to work at Harris Hill during the summer. They used to have the world gliding contests. But I had never been off the ground. My first flight, there was nothing like it. My instructor says to me, 'You know the way back to the field?' 'Oh yes!' And hotshot me, I pointed and he laughed. He turned the plane up in a vertical and he pointed right over to the home field. I was really embarrassed. [*Laughs*] Eventually I went through training, and the day came when we taxied out in the

---

[8] *PT-17s-* Most Tuskegee pilots first trained in PT-17 Stearman aircraft; 'PT' meant 'primary trainer.' Though 10,000 were built in the 1930s and into the 1940s by Boeing, only two are now known to exist. www.collingsfoundation.org/aircrafts/boeing-pt-17-tuskegee-stearman/

middle of the field. He says, 'Okay, take it around and don't break up the airplane.' That was when I soloed. First time in the air by myself, and the greatest thrill I ever had! The people who even learn to fly today, the first time you are turned loose, you fly by yourself, and it is a big thrill.

Then they transferred us to the Army Air Corps field for basic and advanced training. Our basic trainers were BT-13s, Vultee Vibrators as they were called, where we learned instrument flying and night flying. I had a little trouble in my basic training, because learning to fly instruments, it's like learning to walk blindfolded. You had to navigate and control the airplane solely by your instruments. One particular day I couldn't do anything right. I couldn't hold a heading, and I couldn't hold an altitude. When we came back I had tears in my eyes because I knew that I was washed out. I told the instructor what he could do with his airplane, which wasn't nice. [*Laughs*] When you come back with your instructor, you usually have to stand there and you critique your flight. You have to salute him and then go back to the ready room. I didn't even give him the benefit of that. I just turned on my heel, and like I said, I told him what he could do with his airplane! I went back up to the barracks and started packing my clothes because I knew I had washed out. The next day my name was on the board, and I went back and had a good day. I went to advanced training in T-6s.[9]

---

[9] *advanced training in T-6s*-Mr. Dart continued: 'My kids gave me a ride in a T-6 last year. Remember the airplanes that were advertised that were flying out of the field down in Ballston? They had T-6s down there. I forgot how much it cost, but it must have cost them three or four hundred dollars. My kids gave me a ride in a T-6 after all those years. I got to do a few aerobatics and whatnot. I got to do rolls and loops. It was fun and I appreciated it.'

North American AT-6C-NT Texan trainer, 1943. Credit: USAF, public domain.

When I first got to advanced training, the instructor I had was a real short guy. He was just a little over five feet six inches. He was demonstrating how safe the airplane was. He rolled it on its back. The T-6s didn't have an inverted fuel system, so the engine quit. I'm strapped in this seat and the ground is coming up. He is gliding this thing upside down. I see the trees coming up! Pretty soon he flips the airplane back over. He restarts the engine and said, 'See, you had nothing to worry about, because the airplane is safe.' [*Laughs*] For about five minutes I was questioning his method of teaching me to fly. He was a good instructor, and, in fact, our training group was the only one to do formation aerobatics—nothing exotic like you see at air shows, but loops and formations.

I finally graduated from advanced, and eventually I got my commission on November 3rd, in 1943. We transitioned into P-40s. That was an experience, because in the military in those days, when you transitioned into another airplane, they just showed you how to start the engine and gave you some of the air speeds that you should fly at for approach and take-off. And away you go; there is no instructor in there with you! Nowadays in the military you have to go to school and simulators. That's why they require everyone to have a college education in the Air Force today—because it is very complicated. There are lots of buttons to push. If you ever get to see the cockpit of those fighters nowadays, you just wonder how the guys ever have time to do anything but just watch all these little screens [*laughs*] and push all these little buttons and whatnot. Doing the things they have to do is very complicated. My class [size] fell as we graduated. We took our transitioning into this one beat-up P-40 that they had there.

Curtiss P-40Fs near Moore AAF, 1943. 'The lead aircraft in a formation of P-40s is peeling off for an 'attack' in a practice flight at the Army Air Forces advanced flying school. Selected aviation cadets were given transition training in these fighter planes before receiving their pilot's wings.' Credit: USAF, public domain.

Then we were sent to Selfridge Field outside of Detroit, Michigan, for overseas training. From there, every day we used to fly up to a field called Oscoda, which is north of Detroit, in the wintertime. That was an experience, because they didn't have very good snow removal systems up there. Sometimes coming in to land it was really an experience if you weren't lined up, if you were a little off line; the next thing you know, you would be going down the runway 'round and 'round like the cars do on the Northway![10] [*Laughs*] It was fun. But a lot of times we'd fly back in snowstorms, so our instrument training was very valuable to us.

To North Africa and Italy

After that we were sent to Patrick Henry and were transferred overseas. We had the good fortune to be on a luxury liner that had been converted to a troop transport, so we had good meals, except that we ran into one big storm, and, well, it wasn't funny, because this one time in the middle of the storm the ship started to roll. Then it got worse, and the next thing you know, the chairs and tables, they weren't bolted down, people were sliding from one side [*laughs*] of the ship to the other; oh, what a mess! You could hear the crockery and the plates falling on the floor, breaking! Well, after about a couple hours of that, we got out of the storm into calmer water, and after nine days we landed in Oran, Morocco. We were sent to the edge of the desert to train for a while.

North Africa and the Mediterranean had been cleared by the summer of 1943, although the opening of a second front in Italy had been hotly debated among the Allied high command. Churchill famously characterized Italy as the 'soft underbelly of Europe,' arguing that it was imperative to take down Mussolini and knock Italy out of the war, and also buy time before the massive cross-channel invasion from England. Hitler would be forced to divert troops to Italy from Russia, and the oil refineries of Romania and industrial targets in southern Germany would be more

---

[10] *like the cars do on the Northway*-Interstate 87 in upstate New York, during treacherous winter conditions.

accessible for Allied air power flying out of Italian bases. Others, such as the U.S. Army Chief of Staff George C. Marshall, opposed it as drawing off too many resources for the cross-channel invasion. The Italian campaign would rage for over 500 days, with the Allies suffering over 300,000 casualties, slogging it out against the Germans up the 'bloody boot'; the Germans would lose more than 430,000 killed and wounded.

The 99th Fighter Squadron, which I was eventually transferred to, had come over earlier. They had fought with the 12th Air Force with the 79th Fighter Group and they had moved to Italy. We got a chance to do some dive bombing and strafing there on the desert and flying under a bridge, which we were told not to do, but we all did it anyhow, just the thrill of it, you know. [*Laughs*] There was nobody around to tell us really what to do. There were no officials, so to speak, except for the people running the field there, so once we got out of sight, [we had fun]. We used to do the same thing at Tuskegee; we used to buzz the people picking cotton in the fields [*chuckles*], stuff like that. There were all kinds of complaints, but people just didn't know how to report us, because if they got a number off the airplane or something, you know, you'd be washed out right away.

Combat

The 99th Fighter Squadron got their first taste of combat in North Africa in April 1943. From there, they moved to Sicily to support the invasion of Italy, and then to the mainland to support combat operations there.

We were put on a C-47 to catch up to the 99th at Capodichino [Field] outside of Naples, Italy, on the day before Vesuvius erupted.[11] Just the weight of the ashes out of that volcano destroyed nearly every airplane on the field, broke the wings off, the tails off; it was a mess. So we didn't have any airplanes to fly, and we had to wait, oh, I guess it was over a week, and they flew in replacements for us. Then they moved us to a little town outside of Naples called Cercola, and we were based there for the first few months. That's where I started my combat career.

*

The first time you find people trying to kill you, it puts you in a different phase in your life. You know, when I was a kid, I used to read all these romantic stories about 'G-8 and his Battle Aces,' about air duels in WWI, when the Germans were flying the Fokkers and the Allies were flying Spads, Sopwith Camels, and stuff like that. Well, our job [at that time] mainly was to do dive bombing and strafing, so we were never more than two or three thousand feet in the air, and you would have to come down from that anyhow to strafe, except when you were dive bombing.

I think it was on my fifth mission when we got a call to relieve some GIs who had been pinned down by the Germans. They told us to go give them some help. We had a new flight leader, and he should have known better, because he had been there about a month or two ahead of us. So he put us in trail, like in a gunnery school formation, you know, everybody nose to tail, but with, you know, some space. So we spotted the target—we went around the first time firing at, I think it was, a German machine gun nest; no return fire, so we went around the second time. I said, 'This isn't right,' because in the rules of combat, if you make the first pass and

---

[11] *the day before Vesuvius erupted*- Mt. Vesuvius most famously erupted on August 26, AD 79, destroying and burying the Roman cities of Pompeii and Herculaneum. Quite active in history many times since, the last major eruption on March 18, 1944, destroyed over six dozen USAAF aircraft and damaged many others.

you don't get any return fire, you just keep going, you come back another day. Well, we went around a third time and the ground opened up—it was like the best Fourth of July sight you've ever seen! They threw everything at us, and it wasn't long before I heard a big 'bang' and the cowling on my plane started peeling off, like somebody peeling a banana. Then another 'bang' and a hole opened up between my feet and the rudder pedals, and another 'bang' behind the cockpit, and the next thing I knew I was counting blades![12] There was a three-bladed prop on the P-40s; they shot out my fuel lines, oil lines, coolant lines, and the engine quit. And since we were strafing, I think I was down under five hundred feet! So I couldn't jump out, because the kinds of 'chutes we had in those days, if you weren't at least two thousand feet, your chances of landing safely weren't too good, because they were kind of slow opening. They didn't pop open like the parachutes do today. So I had to find a field to put the thing down. I figured I had picked a good field—I thought it was a good field; from the air it looked like it was kind of smooth—but it turned out it was a plowed field. So I knew I was going to have to belly land this thing. I reached down, pushed this little lever that locked my harness, and glided toward the field. One wing dropped. I think it was the right wing that caught the ground, and the airplane cartwheeled—a really rough ride. When it came to a stop, I was sitting there, kind of dazed, in the cockpit. I saw these guys running over this wall into the field. It turned out they happened to be GIs—but not from the place where we were relieving. This was another group of guys, who said the Germans had moved out of this field about an hour before. I was sitting there just in the cockpit because both wings were broken off, the engine was out of the mount, and the tail was broken off, and they got me out of the

---

[12] *counting blades*-the engine quits, the propellers slow their rotation to become visible to the pilot

cockpit! They had a medic with them who fixed up my few scrapes and bangs; well, they got me transportation back to my base. I was on crutches I think for about three days, because I was a little sore, before I was back in the air.

*

Nothing else happened until May of 1944, when we had another mission. The Germans had this big railway gun going—I don't know if you ever heard of it, it's on display down at, I forget that place in Maryland, just outside of Washington, where they have all these exhibits of WWII.[13] But anyway, it's a big railway gun, and the Germans would hide it at night in this railway tunnel, which was up over the beachhead at Anzio, and our job was to try to collapse the tunnel and keep this gun bottled up in there.[14] So we started on our run, because this was going to be not a dive, it was going to be to try to skip the bomb into the mouth of the tunnel. Just as we got about halfway there, I heard a 'bang,' and I didn't know what it was, but I found out pretty shortly afterwards, because the next thing I know, I could see flames coming out from under the cowling. Then I said, 'Uh-oh, I better put this down on the emergency field,' back at beachhead there, on the beach. I could see this big black cloud trailing behind me as I made my turn, and the guys were yelling at me to get out, but I couldn't; it was too low to jump out. So I made one circle, and I figured I'd put it down in a bunch of saplings. I thought to cushion my impact, but just as I was approaching, all of a sudden I looked and I saw these 155 'Long Toms' [British artillery] in the midst of the saplings—they were using that as a camouflage spot. And I had to drop my bombs safe, but thankfully I didn't pull the arming wires—there's a wire that goes in

---

[13] *all these exhibits of WWII*- The U.S. Army Ordnance Museum, Fort Lee, VA.
[14] *keep this gun bottled up in there*-To the GIs, this monster gun was known as 'Anzio Annie.' It had a crew of 85 men, sported a barrel more than 70 feet long, and could fire its 283mm 550+ lb. shells over 40 miles.

the little propeller on the end of the bomb that sets up the firing mechanism; when the bomb impacts, its pin pulls and the bomb explodes. Well, I dropped them safe, but I think the guys thought that I was going to bomb them [*laughs*], but the bombs didn't hit them. I found a little dirt road going east of there. I put this thing down on the road. I thought the fire had died down enough, but as soon as I hit, the fire flared up! Also, I had rolled the canopy back and locked it into a detent—that's the way you hold the canopy open on a P-40—but the impact, I guess, dislodged the handle. The canopy slammed forward and jammed, and I said, 'Uh-oh, I'm in trouble.' But I managed to get out of my harness, I got my feet under me, and with my back I popped that canopy off the airplane and I was down the road about an eighth of a mile before it blew up. Again I was rescued, so to speak, by some GIs, and they came out with a 6x6 truck. They took me to the beachhead where the Americans were using this big granary, which the Italians used to store their crops when they harvested them, but they were keeping their trucks inside. That doggone gun came out that night and fired at the ships in the harbor! We were supposed to have destroyed it; I don't know why the guys didn't finish the mission, but that gun was firing that night. Every time one of those shells went off, the truck would jump about six feet off the floor because those shells were about the size of a Volkswagen Beetle, and that's the kind of shells that that gun was firing. They were firing at the ships that were supporting the beachhead. So the next day, of course, the gun wasn't firing, because they pull it back into that tunnel.

The GIs had a beat-up P-40 that had landed there before, and they tried to get it started, but they couldn't get it started. So they gave me a ride back to my base about 50 miles down the coast. I got back to base, I wasn't too banged up this time, and I was back flying the next day.

Anyway, I got back through Rome. Mark Clark had taken Rome, liberated it, and the Germans were on the run.[15] I got back to my base and flew a few more missions. Then, in June, they brought over three other squadrons. Meanwhile, Colonel Davis had gone back to the States; he was my commanding officer early, but they [ordered] him back, because there was a lot of criticism about us— of course, it was all made up, just like it was before we got trained, when one senator said he had done a study and he found out that black people's cranial cavity was too small to hold the knowledge to fly an airplane![16] But, see, he didn't know that black people had been flying ever since everybody else had, because there were two schools in the country, one in Chicago and one in Los Angeles. When they brought the other three squadrons over, we got brand-new P-51s like the one in that picture [*points to photograph on the table*].

---

[15] *Mark Clark*-Commander of the U.S. Fifth Army. Rome was liberated on June 4, 1944, the first Axis capital to fall.

[16] *Colonel Davis*-Benjamin O. Davis was only the fourth black officer to graduate from West Point. As the commander of the Tuskegee Airmen, he had to deal with early Army criticism of underperformance, with the suggestion that black pilots were not capable of performing on a scale with whites. This argument was put to rest when in January 1944, the 99th Pursuit Squadron shot down 12 German fighters in a 2-day period. Benjamin Davis went on to become the Air Force's first black general. See www.greatblackheroes.com.

(L-R) Tuskegee Airmen Clarence Dart, Elwood Driver, Hebert Houston, Alva Temple discuss kill of Me-109, summer 1944, Italy. Courtesy Clarence Dart.

Now this was a P-51 'C' or 'B,' not the 'D's that everybody thinks of [*points to photograph again*] when they talk about P-51s. These were the Razorbacks. But they were good airplanes. In fact, I liked them better than the newer 'D's—to me, they were more maneuverable, it was more like a Spitfire—because the 'D's were heavier and they didn't feel as agile as the 'C's were and I felt comfortable, because I thought you weren't as exposed in these airplanes. In the 'D's you had that bubble canopy, you had that 360-degree view, but, like I said, it was heavier, and I didn't like it, but eventually I was given one and told I had to keep it, and they gave my airplane to my wingman! But anyway–

Our time was up for the day. We talked Mr. Dart into coming back again for another session, right before our Christmas holiday break. He was happy to oblige.

Clarence Dart, Part II

Mr. Dart again drove up to our high school from Saratoga Springs, twenty minutes' drive northward. Some of my senior students had expressed a desire to go to Saratoga themselves and pick him up; others noted that if he could fly a P-40 in a blinding Michigan snowstorm, he could probably make his way back. He did not disappoint, and picked up right where he left off, discussing life on base between the missions in wartime Italy.

Life Between Missions

Hygiene was handled by taking the liners out of our helmets [*gestures to his head*] and getting some stones, and putting the metal helmet on some rocks and starting a little fire to warm up the water for our hygiene. During the summer, what we'd do is take jerry cans of water and sit them out in the sun and let the sun heat up the water. Then we had a contraption that we made that was up on two poles with a rope on it, and when the water heated up, you put the can [*motions upwards, like putting can on the top of the poles*] up there and take the rope—and this is all outdoors—and pull it to get a brief shower. Eventually the Corps of Engineers came around and they erected some tents—they used their water wagons and we got a real good shower, they had a way of heating the water—but that only happened once that I can remember. Most of the time we were on our own as far as our hygiene was concerned.

Of course, maybe you have heard your grandfather or somebody that was in service talk about the meals, about K-rations, C-rations, and 'tropical butter' and 'tropical chocolate'—horrible stuff! [*Smiles*] The butter was just about like axle grease, so it wouldn't melt. The tropical chocolate, I defy anybody [*chuckles*] to put one of those bars in your mouth and try to bite off a piece of it; it was hard! I don't think it even melted in your mouth, but you could grind on it for a while until you got the effect of a candy bar. But also, we got a chance, oh, about every two or three weeks, to travel over to the Mediterranean side, and we could go down to the harbor in Naples and beg ice cream from the sailors. They were very cooperative; sometimes they slipped us a steak or something like that. So it wasn't too bad, except for the K-rations and the C-rations. I guess now they have what they call the 'Meals Ready to Eat' [MREs] for guys that are over in Iraq and Afghanistan, places like that. But I think they are a little better set up than we were.

When the weather started getting kind of rough, in order to keep ourselves warm we made little stoves. We would steal copper tubing [*chuckles*] from down on the line, and [*uses hand motions to depict the setup of the stove*] coil it up, and hook it up to a can of gasoline. As it came down through the tube, we would have a little fire down at the bottom that would heat it up and give us pressure, so that would keep the tent warm until it went out. But it didn't last too long, so you would try to get in your sack as soon as possible. Also during the summer, I remember, of course we had mosquito nettings and stuff like that, but once in a while we would get a visitor, somebody that liked to enjoy our [*chuckles*] sacks with us. You know what a gecko is? They used to have a lot of those things over there, and if the nights got kind of cool, when you go to get into bed, you might have a visitor. You get used to things like that.

But the biggest thing that I remember about Italy, outside of combat—did I mention about the kids? I didn't? Well, in the mess times, those kids would come around with little pails that they had made from discarded cans or something like that. [*Pauses*] Before we put a stop to it, they had been going into these fifty-five gallon drums where all the garbage was thrown, or where we would scrape our mess kits in after dinner. Of course, that was our one big meal during the day; most of the time, we didn't even get breakfast. But it bothered me, and the other guys too, that these kids were diving into that mess of, you know, coffee grounds, grease, and bread crusts, scavenging in there to get something to eat, and if they got a good piece of meat I guess they would take it home. So the way we finally put a stop to it—and it was against the rules, but we didn't care—after we had our meal, we would go back for seconds and rake our mess kits into these kids' little cans. We just couldn't stand to see them diving into all that mess just to get something to eat—that is how horrible it was for a lot of the people over there. After the war got going good, I guess they lost most everything, they couldn't grow anything. It was just horrible to think what war does to people, especially people on the losing end, and they lose practically everything.

*

The missions evolved with the nature of the war as the Allies gained more ground, and the airmen found themselves assigned to escort heavy bombers deep into enemy territory. The pilots were ordered to stay close to the bombers at all costs, and soon earned a reputation for not turning away to chase after enemy 'kills,' at great peril, in many cases, to themselves. While the myth that they 'never lost a bomber to the enemy' persists (due to sensationalistic wartime journalism and subsequent repetition), the fact is that they lost far fewer than other fighter escort units.[13]

'You'll go with the bombers'

But that was when we were based at Cercola a few miles away from Naples. That was when I was in the 12th Air Force and we were flying dive bombing and strafing missions until the middle of, I think, June of 1944, and then they transferred the group over to the other side, the Adriatic side, where our field was at Ramitelli. This was when we started flying long-range escort for the bombers, which was a whole new aspect of the war for us, because we hadn't been trained or told about how to escort bombers. But we soon figured it out, because a lot of things we had to learn on our own, just like I told you about dive bombing and strafing before.

The reason why we got our reputation was when we first got over there [to Italy], we used to take the bombers to the 'IP,' which is the Initial Point, where they start the bomb run to the target, and then pick them up when they came off the target. We wouldn't go all the way to the target, but then Colonel Davis said, 'From now on, you'll go with the bombers through the whole mission,' because the Germans were sending their fighters up into their own flak— they were getting desperate. Our mission was to keep the fighters off the bombers, and not to disrupt the formation, because when the bombardier took over the airplane at the Initial Point, he flew the bomber through the Norden bombsight. Once he started on a target, he couldn't deviate because he's figuring out the wind drift and everything, so the bombs will hit where they're supposed to; that Norden bombsight was flying the airplane. They couldn't deviate from the course because once they were on the line to the target, they were compensating for wind drift, all that kind of stuff, so that when they dropped the bombs, they would be as close to the target as possible. Large targets, like railroad yards and stuff like that, the accuracy wasn't as important, but sometimes if they were trying to hit a specific target, like a building, that the intelligence had pointed out was a prime target, they tried to be as close and accurate as possible. There were a lot of stories about that Norden bombsight, where they can drop a bomb from so many thousand feet into a pickle barrel. Well, that didn't happen; they missed a lot of times.[17]

The flak around the oil fields and the factories was very intense. After the first mission, Colonel Davis told us, 'From now on you are going to go with the bombers all the way through the mission.' [*Long pause*] It didn't always work, but that was our mission—we kept the Germans off the bombers. At first they didn't want us, but toward the end, they started asking for us as an escort, because we protected them to and from the missions. Of course, we couldn't do anything about the flak, though. In fact, we lost some of our own guys getting hit by flak.

I'm trying to think how I can describe escorting bombers through the flak. It made for a very intense, intense situation. Of course we were always maybe two or three thousand feet—well, maybe not quite that high—above the bombers. But you could hear the bursts of the flak [*pause*], and you could see the bursts, and you were just wondering when you were going to get hit. You could see some of the bombers when they got hit, especially before they drop their bombs [*pause*]—it was a horrible sight. Well, you didn't see anything except a big bright flash, then you looked again, but there

---

[17] *Norden bombsight*-The physics involved in dropping a bomb from thousands of feet to hit a target on the ground are astoundingly complicated. Carl Norden, a Swiss-born engineer, developed a 50 lb. analog computer that was so valued by the U.S. military that it invested 1.5 billion in 1940 dollars in it (for comparison, the Manhattan Project came in at around 3 billion). Bombardiers went to school for months to learn how to use it; it was installed in the bombers under armed guard and set to self-destruct upon the crashing of the aircraft. Unfortunately, its accuracy was highly questionable, given all of the combat conditions and high altitudes; the bombardier also had to be able to visually sight the target. See www.ted.com/talks/malcolm_gladwell for an interesting discussion.

is nothing there. Sometimes, if the bomber didn't blow up, you would see guys jumping out, or sometimes when you did get a good look at some of the bombers, all you would see is just, like, streamers, you know, when you go to Fourth of July and you see these things blow up in the air. That's just what you'd see from the bombers, you know; ten or twelve guys are gone.

Our main mission was to keep the German fighters off the bombers, because early on, the Germans were taking a big toll because they had a very good air force. They had the experienced fliers, ones who had fought through the Spanish Revolution and their attacks on troops in Russia and Poland.[18] But after our bombers started blowing up their oilfields and whatnot, they were getting short on supplies. But we never did blow up all the manufacturing facilities, because the Germans were smart enough to move them into the mountains and places where the bombers couldn't reach them.

*

Our missions started getting longer—we started flying into Poland and Romania. Well, Ploesti was in Romania, and that was one of the worst missions I have ever flown. That was a long mission, a little over six hours. [Pause]

Have you ever seen a cockpit of an airplane? Do you know how much room is in there? Not a lot. I had to explain to some little kids one time that you can't get up and walk around like a commercial airline or something. It was very confining; you had a lot of stuff on, especially in the wintertime. There was hardly any room to move your arm sometimes. The parachute packer, he put that cylinder for the dinghy packs in the middle, but just squirming around in the cockpit trying to get comfortable, that thing would wind up

---

[18] *through the Spanish Revolution*-The Spanish Civil War, 1936-1939, where the Germans assisted the forces of General Francisco Franco and his fascists, testing their air force and refining their tactics.

in one corner [*chuckles*], and when you got back from a mission, you were pretty sore because it always seemed to come up at an angle at you; it seemed like you were always sitting on the rim of it!

I remember one time a kid asked how we went to the bathroom. Well, we had what is called a 'relief tube.' In the summertime you could access the darn thing, but in the wintertime, when you had all the stuff on, you couldn't access it. So you tried not to have too many liquids in your system when you went off on a mission because you couldn't reach the relief tube. It was uncomfortable, and if you couldn't make it you had to suffer the consequences [*chuckles*]; you didn't smell too good when you got back to base.

It was very cold when you got up to around 25,000 feet; you know, the higher you go, the temperature would drop. We had some heat; we had switched over from P-40s to '51s when we went into the 15th Air Force—there was some heat in the airplane from just one side, I think it was from the left side. That foot would be warm, but after about a half hour or so your right foot would have no feeling in it! So you would just cross it over to the left side [*laughs*] until you got your right foot thawed out. Also, there was another thing. The parachute packer would pack the dinghy—there was a, we called it a dinghy, but it was an inflatable boat in a pack under the parachute. It was blown up by a CO^2 cylinder. If you had to ditch in the water, and you survived the impact, you would grab this little lanyard and pull it and that would allow this CO^2 cylinder to blow up the dinghy. You would crawl in that until somebody came to rescue you. But in the '51, not too many survived the impact because the airplane was just like a submarine; once it hit, it would just go right under. [*Chuckles*] I came very close. That is why I believed somebody was watching over me. I'm trying to make this as cohesive as possible. [*Pause*]

Flying up there, especially in wintertime, going up over the Alps, sometimes we would have to break up the bomber formations and have them circle and take the bombers through the pass, just to get them to the other side of the Alps, because we would get into what they call 'ice fog.' You couldn't see anything, and if you couldn't fly instruments, you didn't know up or down. A couple of times I saw contrails that were going straight down [*makes a downward hand motion*], and you begin to wonder, 'Was that guy going straight down or the way you should be going?' But I was pretty good; after my experiences in training, I got to be a pretty good instrument pilot. So I never had to succumb to vertigo. Some people would, you know, just lose their sense; if they didn't know how to fly instruments, they would lose their sense of whether they were up or down or making a turn, and we lost some people that way. They lost their sense of direction, and the airplane would stall out on them or something, and you would see this contrail going straight down, and in the Alps, you know, it didn't take long before you hit something. But once we got on the other side of the Alps, we would finish the mission.

*

Ploesti's oil refineries were a major source of the lifeblood of the Reich. In 1943, low-level Allied raids from North Africa ended in disaster for B-24 bombers and their crews. Allied planners realized there would be no quick knockout blow; rather a 'rinse and repeat' approach had to be cultivated. As the Allies advanced towards more accessible airfields in eastern Italy, the distance lessened but the risk did not.

We were talking about Ploesti a few minutes ago. That was one of the worst missions I have ever been on. The Germans had about two rings of anti-aircraft guns around the oil fields there at Ploesti, and when the smoke from the flak blew together, there was just one big black cloud in the sky. You could see the bomber formations going in one side, and then there would be big holes in the formation as they came out the other side, and you knew that a lot of them got hit. After they got off the target, we would have to go around and round up the bombers that had straggled away from the formations, and take the long trip back home. Like I said, those missions were at least six hours.

Then we had a strafing mission in Athens, Greece—that was a long mission; we lost a couple guys on that mission. Intelligence would tell us where the headquarters of the German group was, and that was our job to strafe those places. I did not like strafing missions too much. I remember we had one mission around the shores of Lake Balaton.[19] The Germans were retreating, and what they would do was have civilians in the long line of guns and whatever they were moving, as they were trying to get back to Germany. Of course, our orders were to hit anything moving, and we would go down there and make a pass, and they would have horses pulling some of their artillery pieces, and you would see the horses lying on the ground and kicking and whatnot. You can imagine what kind of sound that was. I think we must have hit some of the civilians too, but it was our job to do it, and I had to be sort of counseled; because I didn't think that if they had civilians in those convoys that we should be strafing them. But they tell you this is war. I can remember one time, before I became a flight leader, I was flying wing with a guy who was a flight leader and we hit a motorcycle, one of those side-car motorcycles. I can remember that thing looked like somebody just took it and tossed it up into the air [*makes upward hand motion*]. We got to see the results of that; we got a Jeep and went back up the road. This was when we were flying P-40s. But I just think about how horrible war is, and what you are forced to do against your own will to accomplish a mission.

You just have to adopt a fatalistic view about what you have to do and what is going to happen to you, like I told you last week

---

[19] *Lake Balaton*-Western Hungary.

about my two crashes and getting shot down twice. I remember one time coming back after we had been on a mission to Vienna—and this time it was just a milk run, because although we had flak, we didn't run into any enemy fighters or anything.[20] So we were coming back, we go to the edge of the Adriatic on the Yugoslavia side, and we were just getting ready to tell the bombers that we were going to leave them. We were on the left side of the bombers, so I dropped down and slid under the belly of the lead bomber—to come up beside the pilot side, because we couldn't raise them on the radio—to tell them we were leaving, and that they were safe to go back to their base. I felt a shudder, and I told my wingman, I said, 'Cut the playing around out!' Because just for stress relief sometimes, we tapped wingtips or something like that, which is against the rules! [*Chuckles*]

But my wingman said, 'I wasn't doing anything, I am back where I am supposed to be!'

So when we got back to the field, my crew chief said, 'Oh my goodness, you guys were in it again today.'

I said, 'No, it was just a milk run.'

He said, 'Well, look at this!'

I don't know how I didn't see it in the air, but there was a line of bullet holes from the [*points left*] left wing tip on a diagonal right across down the wing behind my cockpit [*points behind him*] and the tail sections! My airplane was out of commission for about two weeks until they got new parts. In fact, they had to put a whole new tail section on it. I think when the sleepy belly gunner or one of the guys in one of the Plexiglas side windows had seen me or the silhouette of my airplane, he thought maybe I was an Me-109 or a

---

[20] *just a milk run* in World War II airman lingo, a milk run was an easy round-trip mission with little or no enemy resistance, an analogy taken from the old-time dairy practice of the milkman delivering bottles of milk to one's door.

Focke-Wulf 190 and he let me have a burst! [*Laughs*] I still don't know to this day what caused him—he must have been asleep and woke up, and all of a sudden, the reflex, you know—to take a shot at me. I put in a complaint, but nothing was ever done about it. Those were things that happened all the time in the war—friendly fire. You read the things in the paper about in Iraq, about the guys getting in trouble by killing or dropping bombs on their own troops. But war is a dangerous thing, and I have always said when I got back, I said something has got to be done. People should not be doing this, because too many people get killed for no reason at all. A lot of civilians, especially the civilian population, especially when you hit targets in populated areas, you don't always hit the target that you are supposed to hit. Sometimes you are killing people that do not deserve to be killed.

*

Let me tell you some of the dumb things that I did. We were coming back from a mission one time, and it was a nice sunny day; we did not have any encounter with the enemy. We were letting down from about 25,000 feet, and in a '51, what you were supposed to do every now and then is gun the engine to clear the plugs, otherwise they could foul out, and this is what happened to me. We had just gotten to the Adriatic side by Yugoslavia, and then all of a sudden the plane got real quiet and I started counting blades—naturally, the engine had quit! I just had not cleared the engine, because, you know, after a while, I guess you get kind of lackadaisical about things. The engine had quit and we were just starting to go across the Adriatic! Now the P-51 is a nice airplane and it glides for a long ways, but to this day, I just say the Lord was on my side, because I fought that engine all the way across the Adriatic! Now I was not supposed to glide that far, and just as we got to the other side, the engine finally caught on! Meanwhile I had dropped my gear to let the Germans below know I was going to land on the beach and

I was going to be a prisoner of war. Well, that did not mean anything to them! [*Laughs*] Just as I got the engine started there was a big BLAM, and so I took off [*makes a peeling away motion to the left*] to go back to our base, which is on the other side of the Adriatic, there at Ramitelli. Our runway ran right down to the water's edge [*gestures across body at a diagonal motion*]. When I landed, my crew chief said, 'Oh, you've been in it again!'

I said, 'No!'

He says, 'Well, look at this!'

There was a hole about the size of a basketball [*uses hands to show size of hole*] in the wing wood that could have caused that wing to fold up, but I just think the Lord was with me that day.

Berlin

Another time, my last mission was to Berlin. This was March 23, in 1945.[21] They had 'maximum effort,' where every airplane in the 15th Air Force was up that day—all the bombers and all the fighters they could get in the mission to Berlin. We were assigned to a group of bombers, and when we reached a certain point, we were supposed to leave and go back to base and another group was supposed to come up and relieve us. Well, they never showed up, so we had to continue on to Berlin with this group of bombers. The

---

[21] *This was March 23, in 1945-* This dramatic mission was actually on March 24. *'Forty-three P-51 Mustangs led by Colonel Benjamin O. Davis escorted B-17 bombers over 1,600 miles into Germany and back. The bombers' target, a massive Daimler-Benz tank factory in Berlin, was heavily defended by Luftwaffe aircraft, including Fw 190 radial propeller fighters, Me-163 rocket-powered fighters, and 25 of the much more formidable Me-262s, history's first operational jet fighter. Pilots Charles Brantley, Earl Lane, and Roscoe Brown all shot down German jets over Berlin that day. For the mission, the 332nd Fighter Group earned a Distinguished Unit Citation.'* Source: www.everworld.com/tuskegee/332dfightersquadron.htm, via en.wikipedia.org/Tuskegee Alrmen.

Germans sent over their jet fighters that they had developed, the Me-262s, and you could see them coming [*uses swooping hand gestures to depict the position and movements of Me-262s*].[22] They were way up above us, and then, when they started down to attack, the exhaust from their engine was just like a streak of black in the sky. So they hit a few bombers, and I got on the tail of one of them. I dropped my tanks, and then all of a sudden I realized my engine had quit; I'd forgotten to switch to my internal tanks![23] [*Laughs*] I was right on the tail of this guy, and I guess he sensed I was back there. All of a sudden there was a big cloud of black smoke and he was gone—he just disappeared! That's how fast those things were.

Messerschmitt Me 262A at the National Museum of the United States Air Force. Credit: USAF, public domain.

But our group shot down three of them that day, because they made the mistake of slowing down to fight with us. Their turn radius was so large at speed that in order to fight with us, they had to

---

[22] *the Me-262s-* Messerschmitt Me 262, the world's first combat jet-powered aircraft.
[23] *I dropped my tanks-* auxiliary fuel tanks carried by aircraft externally on long-distance missions; they would be jettisoned to reduce drag and provide 'catch-up' power.

slow down, but then it was to our advantage. When they slowed down—because our airplanes could turn inside their circle—we shot down three of them that day. Of course, I wasn't one of them; I was a dummy. I just got so excited because I hadn't seen a fighter, a German plane, in so long, and just that one little mistake in that short length of time cost me [a possible kill]!

After we got back to the base, my commanding officer says, 'You've had it, you've been over here long enough, you've had enough excitement, you've got to go home.' But I told him, 'No, the war's almost over, I want to finish the war,' you know? [*Pauses*] He said, 'No, you've got to go home.' [*Shakes head*] So I said okay; I packed up my kit and got a ride on the 6x6 back to Naples, where the replacement depot was, but I didn't sign in. I went AWOL [*chuckles*].[24] So I was roaming around Naples, you know, and I was getting ready to go someplace else. One of the guys who was back at the base happened to come over—I guess he was going to a rest camp—and he said, 'They're looking all over for you—if you don't hurry up and sign out and go home, they're going to court-martial you!' [*Laughs*] And so I signed in, and I got a C-47, no, it was a DC-4, and I went to LaGuardia in New York in April of '45. I got leave to go home for a couple of weeks, and then they transferred me back to Tuskegee, where they made me an instructor—an instrument instructor. That only lasted a couple of months, because they closed the field at Tuskegee and sent everybody up to Columbus, Ohio, at Lockbourne Field. And there things really slowed down and it was very boring, because, since our group was still overseas, there was no place for us to go. There were no jobs on the base—I mean, there were a few jobs, but the other groups weren't accepting us.

So, I finally went home and went to school: Aero Industries Technical Institute, out in Oakland, California. And when I finished

---

[24] *I went AWOL*-absent without leave, a punishable offense.

there, I came back home and went to work. Well, I didn't get a job right away. I got married, and then I went down to General Electric. I walked in the door, and the receptionist said, 'We don't have any jobs for you.' I had just gotten inside the door and that's what I was confronted with! I didn't even get a chance to ask her, you know, were they hiring anybody. [*Laughs*] One of the interviewers just happened to be walking by and he heard her, so he caught my eye and he beckoned me with his finger, and I followed him into his office. He said, 'Let me see what you've got.' I had my portfolio with me, and he looked at it, my school records and everything, and said, 'When can you start?' I said, 'As soon as possible.' He said, 'Okay, show up Tuesday morning.' Well, Monday was a holiday, but I got paid for it—my first day at GE and I didn't even work and I got paid for it, because it was a holiday! That was in April of 1948. I went to work for GE and stayed there for almost 40 years.

I had several positions at GE. First I went to work for the General Engineering Lab, and then they transferred me to Flight Test. I couldn't wait to get to work in the morning. That's the best place I'd ever worked in my life. It was a very interesting place. We did all kinds of things there. They had all kinds of airplanes—B-29s, B-17s, B-35s. They had a jet that was designed by the British, but Martin Aircraft was building them under license, and we were doing some work on that, and improving. And I was at Flight Test for I guess two years, and then they closed the place. We were doing a lot of repair work, along with other test work, which we were doing for customers. In fact, we had one of the early 707s, and my job was to design a stable platform for it. This was like a telescope, but it was a device that would read the signatures of missiles coming through the atmosphere so that you could tell whether it was really a missile, or a decoy. But in examining the airplane—the airplane had just come from a place down in Birmingham, I think it was—and they did some repair work, and so we called a pilot and showed him what had happened; those guys had put rivets in that were too long, but instead of heading the rivets, like you were supposed to do, they just bent them over! [*Laughs*] And the blood just drained out of that fellow's face, because, well, it was really a hazard. If any real stress had been put on that airplane, it would've come apart in the air.

After Flight Test, I was transferred to Knolls Atomic Power Lab outside of Ballston Spa, where they run test reactors for either submarines or ships. Very interesting work, but for the years that I worked there, you didn't dare get caught talking about what you did there. Well, like I said, I retired, and so, that's it. That's the end of the 'Clarence Dart' saga. [*Laughs*]

*

It was time for a question and answer session with the students.

Student: How did you feel about Eleanor Roosevelt before you went overseas?

Oh! She was one of the reasons that they finally decided to train black pilots. Our chief, Chief Anderson, he gave her a ride in a Piper—I think that's what it was, a Piper Cub. But she went back and she told Franklin that we could fly just like anybody.

I don't like to get into a lot of arguments about what black people can do or what they have done. But, if you do the research, just like all the war pilots I've told you about, black men have served in every war that this country has ever fought—from Crispus Attucks on up to this day.[25] Back in the Civil War, there were 18 Congressional Medals of Honor given out to black soldiers. But people conveniently forget all of that stuff—from Bunker Hill to the Spanish-

---

[25] *Crispus Attucks*-victim of the Boston Massacre, March 5, 1770.

American War—and of course you saw the movie about the Massachusetts 54th?[26] In fact, even during World War I, there was a destroyer that was manned, officers and sailors, by blacks. Of course, there's a lot of black history. We did the first open-heart surgery with Dr. Daniel Hale Williams, and the guy that invented the most annoying things to people who drive cars—the stop light—Garrett Morgan. And he also invented the first breathing device that they used to rescue some people when they were putting in a water line out in, I think it was Cleveland, Ohio, out into the lake—they rescued some guys that were in the tunnel; they used his breathing device! And what about the doctor who invented the way to preserve blood plasma? But over the years, people like that knuckle-headed senator, who said that black people's cranial cavity was too small to hold the knowledge to fly an airplane, well, he demonstrated that he was way behind the times, because we had people that had flown cross-country trying to prove that black pilots should be trained for the war and World War II! And it continues to this day—

Interviewer: What about the white bomber crews that you escorted?

Well, early on they didn't want us, because they had listened to the propaganda, but when they found out that they weren't getting shot up by the Messerschmitts and 190s when we were escorting them, then they started requesting us for coverage. In fact, a couple of times—you know what photo reconnaissance is? They had a stripped down P-51, and I had to escort two of those things on two different times. You were all by yourself, deep in enemy territory. But those guys, their airplanes were very fast, because they were all

---

[26] the Massachusetts 54th-*Glory*, 1989 winner of three Academy Awards, depicting an all-black regiment's assault on a Confederate stronghold.

stripped down, and all they had were cameras in them, and it was tough trying to keep up with them—once they got their pictures, they just took off, of course, and myself and my wingman, we would just be left out in the middle of Germany someplace, trying to get back home. [*Laughs*]

Student: Were you restricted from any white establishments?

Well, that was the norm back in those days—up to World War II. In fact, it didn't end until, let's see, 1954.[27] With my background, being brought up in Elmira, New York, we didn't know what [segregation] was, because in my neighborhood, everybody was mixed. We had white kids that came to my house for dinner, or I'd go to their homes for dinner, and there was never any of that kind of stuff, you know, generally. Not until we got below—well, I can remember, going south in the summer to visit my cousins, of course; my father worked on the railroad. He could get passes to go on different railroads. When you got to Washington, D.C., whatever car you were in, you had to go get in one separate car for black people [*pauses*] to go south of Washington, across the Mason-Dixon Line. You couldn't ride on the sleepers, and you couldn't go into the dining car. So my mother and grandmother, what they would do was fix up a basketful of food that would last for a day and a half to travel to South Carolina. That was in those days—

Student: Was there any difference in the way you were treated here and when you were in Italy?

---

[27] *it didn't end until 1954*-The armed services were officially desegregated in 1948; Mr. Dart refers to the landmark Supreme Court decision of *Brown v. Board of Education of Topeka* in which the Court declared state laws establishing separate public schools for black and white students to be unconstitutional, paving the way for further desegregation.

Well, the Italians, they weren't prejudiced. Prejudice was only in this country. In fact, when the war was over, and they brought everybody back by boat, and they got off the boat, there were signs saying 'Coloreds,' you know. You'd been overseas for almost two years, you'd go to an army base, and the German prisoners of war were treated better than you were; it was a hard pill to swallow. [*Pauses, expressing sadness*] Because even if you went to a movie theater—this was back in '45 and later—you'd go to a theater and they'd have a place for black soldiers to sit, you know, in the movie theater. And you couldn't use the PX. You'd have to use a different PX; they had one for blacks and one for whites.[28] In fact, they had formed a bomb group, the 477th Bomb Group, B-25s, and it was somewhere out in the Midwest, in Kentucky or someplace, and these guys weren't going to have any of that nonsense. They went to an officers' club, and even in those days the army had said that anybody who was an officer could go into any officers' club. But at this particular field, I think it was Freeman Field, the guys went to the club, and they tried to keep them out, and they went in anyhow. And because one guy happened to rush past one of the officers at the club, they court-martialed thirteen of them, I think it was. But the people who held on to that segregation eventually were court-martialed themselves. Plus, their orders were sent around to all the military bases that there was not to be any segregation of all officers.[29]

---

[28] *you couldn't use the PX*-Post Exchange, or the place on a military installation where consumer goods could be purchased.

[29] *there was not to be any segregation of all officers*- The Tuskegee Airmen of the 477th challenged the all-white officers' club at Freeman Army Air Field in Seymour, Indiana. Scores of black officers were arrested and three were court-martialed over several incidents in April 1945. Forty years later, their records were expunged; the incidents were regarded as an important step in the eventual integration of the military, and a spark for the fledgling civil rights movement.

Student: How do you feel about the new war—the war in Iraq. How do you feel about that?

Oh! We shouldn't be there—we shouldn't have gone without the cooperation of the United Nations. Now, it hasn't been that long ago when the president said that Iraq was a direct threat to the United States, and I looked at my wife and I said, 'What's he talking about?' And I said, 'You know Saddam Hussein was a bad guy, but he doesn't—after the first Gulf War—he doesn't have a navy, he doesn't have an air force. He's probably got a big army, but how can he reach the United States? He doesn't have any missiles. And I don't know how he could be a direct threat to the United States. I said, 'All they're going to do is get a lot of people killed for nothing.' And we did—we went over there, and of course, with our airplanes and technology, it didn't last long. Two weeks, I think it was? I think it lasted for two weeks, but look at what's happened since then—because I think we should have insisted that the UN, that since Saddam is guilty of all those things against, what do they call it?

Student: Crimes against humanity.

Yes. Since he committed all these things, then it's up to the UN to take care of it. We shouldn't be the policemen of the world. Our military is spread so thin now, if a couple other big countries wanted to jump on us, we'd be in big trouble! We've got people in Afghanistan, Korea—all over—islands, Guam, et cetera. We shouldn't be spread like that. And my basic thing that I tell my young grandchildren, I say, George Washington, in his Farewell Address, at one point he said, 'Beware of foreign entanglement.' I think those were the last words he said—'Beware of foreign entanglement.' But

I don't know what's happened in this country. We've exported out technology, and you go to buy something in a store, you look at the labels—all our textiles and clothing are coming from overseas. It shouldn't have been that way! But the CEOs, you've seen what's happened to a lot of these CEOs, like the guy that gave his wife a million dollar birthday party, and built, I don't know, five or six million dollar homes around the world, but he was a big crook![30] I remember when the president of SONY came over [from Japan], and he said, 'You're paying your CEOs too much money.' Now this was by a man that has one of the biggest electronic firms in the world. He said, 'You're paying your CEOs too much money!' Look at what [a famous CEO] got when he retired from [a Fortune 500 company] [*laughs*]—he did give back some of it, of course; his wife, I guess, got the other half for her shenanigans. [*Laughs*] What—why do they deserve that? If you run a large company, sure, you set the goals and you hire people to help you attain those goals, but why should one guy get as much money as it would take to hire maybe a hundred workers? It's not fair, you know, for a lot of money to be all in one, or among certain groups of people. But I'm not a communist or anything. [*Laughter in room*]

I got so mad at professional sports too, a while back, and so I don't watch football and basketball like I used to. And especially the rappers—I saw a piece in one of the Sunday papers where one guy is a billionaire already! You know, of course he branched out into a line of clothing and whatnot, but, I know my kind of music, and what kids like today—

Student: What kind of music do you like?

---

[30] *but he was a big crook*- Mr. Dart may be referring to the Enron scandal, which broke in 2001; our interview was in 2003.

Oh, I'm a jazz man. You know, Duke Ellington, Count Basie—

Student: You'd get along with my grandfather.

Yes, [*laughs*] I don't laugh at the kids nowadays, but when I was growing up, the Elks Club used to have dances for teenagers a lot, and you'd learn how to dance, you'd learn how to dance with a girl. [*Laughter in room*] You [*pointing to male students*] take a girl to a dance and you might not find her until the evening is almost over; you're out there, jumping up and down [*jerks shoulders and arms up and down repeatedly, to much laughter*] in one spot! That's not dancing! When I was in the cadets, we used to go to the Institute when they had dances for the cadets, and, of course, the rule was, 'no buckle-polishing'—you couldn't dance close, more than six inches closer to a girl [*shows distance with hands*]. But at least you could dance with her and talk to her, and put a bug in her ear, or something, you know... [*much laughter in room*] Well, I mean romancing, you know. Convince her that you were the one for her! But I know times have changed—I've raised eight kids, I know what it's like; six girls and two boys. The only hard thing was putting them through college.

Student: Did you take advantage of the G.I. Bill when you came back from the war?

Most people with half a brain, that's what they did, but some people didn't.

Student: Why didn't you try to be an airline pilot, or wouldn't they let you?

Oh, no; we tried. But [my reasoning on it] was that they had a lot of bomber pilots coming back, guys that had flown multi-engine airplanes. We did have two guys that were vice presidents of airlines—one guy was vice president of Eastern Airlines, and another guy was vice president of another airline, I've forgotten which one—but we had a lot of guys who were doctors and lawyers, bank presidents. [*Pauses*] Yes, there were a lot of successful people who took advantage of the G.I. Bill. Well, it was the only thing to do, the smartest thing to do. I don't know if they offer that to the guys coming back from Iraq. [*Someone answers in the affirmative*] They do? I'm glad to hear it, because veterans for the most part have gotten the shaft, especially as far as health care is concerned. That's kind of tragic...

Now out of time after two days of conversation, we wished Mr. Dart and his wife and family a Merry Christmas and holiday season. It was the last time that we saw him. On March 30, 2007, he and his fellow surviving Tuskegee Airmen were presented with the Congressional Gold Medal by then President George W. Bush, who gave them a long overdue salute. Clarence Dart passed away at age 91 in February 2012.

After Mr. Dart passed, I had the opportunity to speak with his son, Warren Dart, who drove up to my classroom to meet me to share more stories and photographs of his dad.

'Though my dad liked to talk to young people, there were some things he couldn't share. Once, he told me of a time when he was returning from a mission to base and spotted a German truck parked behind some trees. He circled around, dove in, and opened up on them. As he attacked the German soldiers, it occurred to him that they had pulled off the road to have their lunch. They were killed, and it's something that probably bothered him for the rest of his life.'

The Tuskegee Airmen Fight Song

Contact –
Joy stick back –
Sailing through the blue
Gallant sons of the 99th –
Brown men tried and true
We are the Heroes of the Night –
To hell with the Axis might
FIGHT! FIGHT! FIGHT! FIGHT!
Fighting 99th.
Rat-tat, Rat-tat-tat –
Down in flames they go
The withering fire of the 99th –
Sends them down below
We are the Heroes of the Night –
To hell with the Axis might
FIGHT! FIGHT! FIGHT! FIGHT!
Fighting 99th.
Drink up, Drain your cup –
To those daring men
Flying torch of flame, Oh GOD–
Red White and Blue – Amen.
For We Are –
Heroes of the Night
To Hell with the Axis might
FIGHT! FIGHT! FIGHT! FIGHT!
Fighting 99th WINGS![14]

*

John Weeks holds a photo portrait of himself and four of his friends, cap-
tioned, 'THE FIRST FIGHTER ESCORTED PHOTO RECON MISSION TO BERLIN'
(L to R) Lt. Schultz, Lt. Belt, Lt. Weeks, Capt. Batson, Lt. Davidson
13th Photo Recon Squadron – Mt. Farm Airfield, England
Credit: Wayne Clarke, NYS Military Museum.

CHAPTER THREE

The Reconnaissance Man

John Weeks sits in a chair in a public library where he volunteers to teach business investment classes at night. He appears with an aura of contentedness at being able to share his experiences, certainly grateful for the opportunity to remember his friends, generations after they were all 'touched by fire.' To the camera he holds up a framed photograph. Five young men are smiling for the camera, posing in front of a plane, standing on a perforated steel Marston Mat. 'Three out of the five men in this photograph did not survive the war; there was only one other survivor besides myself.'

In 1994, John was contacted by 'two gentlemen who run a museum in Plzen, Czech Republic, which is very active in gathering artifacts and information on World War II historical events that took place over their country, including the fate of airmen that were killed and perhaps missing in that area.' They got his name from his former commander.

'These men were particularly interested in a mission I took on April 26, 1945—which may very well have been the last photo reconnaissance mission of the war. I'm not sure why they were so very interested in that

particular mission, but I have the feeling that one of them may have been flying one of the jets that came up after me on that mission.'

*

John G. Weeks

I was born on March 7, 1922, and brought up in western New York State in a little town called Lyons. My father was a fruit farmer there and I worked on the farm, of course. After high school, I attended college in Grove City, Pennsylvania, where I majored in industrial engineering, which was a combination of business and engineering. I went into the army during my junior year.

I was 19, and I was playing bridge at college with some fraternity brothers of mine, and we had the radio on and we heard about Pearl Harbor. We couldn't believe it. I don't think we had any idea of the significance of what was happening, but, as I say, it was just kind of an unbelievable thing; we even wondered if it was a fake or not.

Shortly thereafter, after being turned down by the Marine Air Corps and the Navy Air Corps because of a misalignment of my back teeth, I was accepted and enlisted in the Army Air Corps. I was sworn in at the post office in Pittsburgh and immediately left for basic training at Miami Beach, Florida—where I had my first introduction to the war. We lived in one of the big hotels on the beach, and every morning when we got up, we looked out over the ocean and there would be black smoke on the horizon. It was a little sobering to learn that smoke came from ships that the Germans had torpedoed the night before out in the Gulf Stream right off the coast of Florida. The reason they were able to do that was because we didn't have a blackout in Miami Beach, and so that highlighted the targets that the Germans were after and it made it easy for them. Later, that was corrected.

After about six weeks in Florida, we were shipped to Wittenberg College in Springfield, Ohio. We spent about two months in Wittenberg, where we took a concentrated course—mostly in mathematics, from arithmetic through calculus. I have never worked so hard on academics before or since. Many of the budding cadets washed out at this point. From Wittenberg, we went to Santa Ana Army Air Force Base in California. We spent about six weeks here, with great concentration on astronomy for celestial navigation, and aeronautical engineering—including hydraulics, electrical systems, aerodynamics, and navigation. We also went through altitude chamber training, where they put you in a tank and sucked the air out to simulate altitude, as well as other equipment training. Then we went to Ryan Field in Tucson, Arizona, where we were going to learn to fly at last; I have never had such a thrilling good time in my life.

We flew a Ryan PT-22, which was originally designed in 1930. We had to have nine hours of instruction before we could solo—I had nine hours and three minutes. What a thrill! I just loved it. I had really found a home in the Air Corps.

Then we went to Marana Army Air Field in Arizona, where we flew the BT-13. It was 'affectionately' known as the 'Vultee Vibrator' because it shook so hard in a spin. I never liked the airplane very well, and I don't think many other cadets did either. It was very poor in acrobatics.

From Marana, I was sent to Williams Field in Chandler, Arizona, for my final advanced phase of cadet training. Here we flew the AT-6, which was a delightful plane to fly—very good at acrobatics. We also took a heavy concentration of ground school at Williams Field, where we had already been assigned to fly the Lockheed Lightning P-38—which simply delighted me; that was the plane I wanted. Ground school concentrated almost exclusively on the various systems on the P-38. After a couple of months at

Williams, I graduated as a bright new 2nd lieutenant and had a very coveted pair of pilot's wings.

I stayed right at Williams Field for my transition training into the P-38. We flew lots of lesser airplanes to get used to handling two engines—AT-9s, C-45s, UC-78s, B-25s. Because the P-38 was a single-place plane, the day finally came when they put you in one and simply said, 'Go!' It was quite a transition from 600 horsepower to 3,500 horsepower, from 160 miles per hour to 400 miles per hour in one jump—and all alone!

After Williams, we went to Will Rogers Field in Oklahoma City. Here we learned how to perform our specialty, photo reconnaissance, most of which was done at high altitude—25,000 feet or higher. You see, our mission was much different than that of the ordinary fighter pilot—we flew all alone in planes with no guns, only cameras, and had to survive only on our skill as a pilot and the speed of our planes to evade the enemy. Our training here was a combination of pinpoint navigation and high altitude photography. I think I photographed every tiny little town in the Midwest.

From there we went to Coffeyville, Kansas, for our combat training. I thought I was a pretty good pilot until I got to Coffeyville. Here our instructors were all pilots who had completed their combat missions and had returned to the States as instructors. They were really good. We practiced day after day doing nothing but evasive maneuvers and mock combat; it was very hard work. Our training was cut short, however, because the loss of reconnaissance pilots in Europe was so great during the Normandy invasion that they needed replacements badly.

Overseas

We were rushed overseas on the ocean liner *Île de France*, which made the crossing, unescorted, in five days, landing in Glasgow. We were processed very quickly and rushed to the Mt. Farm air base near Oxford, England.

The reason for the rush was immediately evident. The 13th Photo Recon squadron, to which I was assigned, had only 13 pilots left out of a full complement of 25, and those thirteen were exhausted. There were only five of us replacements—which meant that even with us, the squadron was still far below its full complement. Our mission was to photograph bomb damage of the major cities in Germany and France at that time, also ground movement of troops and so on—we were just trying to keep track of what the Germans were doing, and our bombing missions were based on the photographs that we took.

Our training time was brief, out of necessity, and consisted of very little flying. It was assumed that you knew how to fly and that you knew how to navigate and take pictures, so most of our time was spent talking tactics with the more experienced pilots. Because we flew alone, everybody developed their own tactics, so from talking with them, you sorted out what you thought made the most sense and determined to follow that course. We were also quite short of planes, because whenever you lost a pilot, you lost a plane.

Our early missions were shorter and less dangerous so that we could get the feel of things. I flew nineteen missions, and they were all over.

Reconnaissance P-38 with bold black and white invasion stripes
during the Normandy Campaign.
Credit: USAF. Public domain.

I was assigned an older P-38J, which still had its invasion stripes painted on it. I never liked the plane—it was slow and was not equipped with dive breaks like the newer models. But because the loss of reconnaissance planes was so consistently high, the army tried to keep us equipped with the very latest model planes and equipment. Early on I got a brand-new P-38L with larger engines, dive flaps, rear-facing radar—the whole ball of wax. It was a wonderful airplane—very fast, very maneuverable, and quick to handle.

Let me explain a little about the dive flaps. The P-38 was so powerful, heavy, and streamlined that it would, in a dive, quickly go into compressibility, which made the plane curl under, which would eventually tear the tail off. Once it got into this condition, there was no recovery. The dive brakes were under the leading edge of each wing and were only about two feet long and about two inches wide. When extended with a push of a button, they would immediately pull the nose up and out of compressibility. They had an added bonus, too. In combat, if you were in a tight turn with an enemy plane, the turn would be tightened markedly when you popped these brakes. I'm sure that scared the devil out of many an enemy pilot, because he didn't know for sure whether you had guns or not, and that maneuver would put you right on his tail.

Flying High

I mentioned that each pilot developed his own tactics. Mine developed gradually, of course. I would fly as high as possible, with my limit being 39,000 feet or the bottom of the jet trail [condensation] level—you didn't want to create a jet contrail, because it would point right to you [like a finger]. Though the plane could go higher, thirty-nine thousand feet was my personal limit. Our cockpits were not pressurized, so my body would swell and get very uncomfortable because of the lack of air pressure. My legs would fill out my pants completely, my stomach would become much extended, and my neck would fill up my shirt, even with the top button undone. It was also dangerous because even though we had a pressurized oxygen system, if anything went wrong with it, you wouldn't be able to stay conscious but for a very few seconds—you would never have time to get down to a safe altitude. On the plus side, there were very few enemy planes that could get above you, and flak couldn't touch you that high. So while it was uncomfortable and dangerous, I felt most secure being way up there.

German Messerschmitt Me 163B Komet rocket-propelled fighter at the National Museum of the United States Air Force, Dayton, Ohio.
Credit: USAF. Public domain.

It became more and more precarious as the war proceeded, however. First the Germans developed the Komet, the Messerschmitt 163, solely for the purpose of shooting down photo reconnaissance planes. This was an amazing rocket-powered plane that could climb at 40,000 feet per minute at a 70-degree angle and was very comfortable above 39,000 feet. The one saving grace for us was that it only had an eight-minute fuel supply, which meant that it could fly only by using its engine in short bursts and had to land without fuel. It was very vulnerable to our fighters in its glide mode. I was never attacked by an Me-163 and only saw one at a distance a couple of times.

The only time my plane was hit by enemy fire was on a mission to the Hannover area. If I was lucky enough to have thick clouds at high altitude, my tactic would be to fly just above the tops, quickly dive into the clouds in case of trouble. That was the situation on this day. When I was well over enemy territory, I saw a single plane off to my right going in the opposite direction. The British flew Spitfires on photo recon missions all alone, just like we did; I thought probably that was what the plane was. But it was a long way off, and German Me-109 fighters looked a lot like a Spitfire at a distance. I didn't want to take the chance that it was an Me-109 trying to circle around behind me, so I watched him very carefully.

German ground crew pushes Me-109 onto tarmac, fall 1943, France. Credit: Bundesarchiv, Bild 101I-487-3066-04 via Wikimedia Commons.

All of a sudden I saw tracer bullets going by my canopy! I looked up in my rear view mirror, which was fastened to the canopy about three inches above my head. He was firing at me from behind; I saw him for only a fraction of a second when my rear view mirror disappeared—it had been shot off! I quickly dove into the clouds right below me and made a turn. I flew along for a while and came up for a peek, and my adversary was nowhere in sight. Needless to say, I was much more careful to look all around, all of the time, after that.

About this time, things got really bad, because the Germans had come out with the Me-262 jet fighter. This plane could climb much faster and much higher than our P-38s. Our losses increased alarmingly, mostly due to these new jet fighters. It was at this point that the Air Corps provided us with P-51 fighters to escort the P-38 recon planes. They did not provide us with trained fighter pilots, but told us we would have to do our own escorting. So some of the recon pilots elected to fly the fighters as escort rather than fly the P-38 recon planes—they trained themselves. We used to laugh that the self-trained fighter pilots really weren't all that good, but I'm sure they looked formidable to the enemy. I didn't like the P-51 so elected to stay with the P-38 flying recon.

My worst mission was taken on Christmas Eve 1944. This was during the Battle of the Bulge. The weather had been very bad for about two weeks, and the troops were taking a terrible beating on the ground. On the day before Christmas, the sky cleared completely.[31] Both sides had had two weeks to make repairs on all of their planes, so when things cleared, it was a 'maximum effort' on both sides. It has been estimated that there were 7,000 planes in the air on that day. My mission was to Cologne and then back to the Bulge area. I was alone and was 'jumped' six times on that one mission.

[As I stated] we had very heavy losses; the Germans knew that if they saw one P-38, they pretty well knew that it was a photographic plane and they'd go after us. Sometimes if it was a 'black star' priority, which was a major 'do-or-die' type mission, they

---

[31] *Battle of the Bulge*- Hitler's last gamble to counterattack between the advancing American and British forces in northern France and the Low Countries began on Dec. 16, 1944. After the Normandy landings, the incredible magnitude of American industrial capacity dictated to Hitler that somehow the supply lines had to be cut, and he chose the Ardennes Forest for the avenue of attack in the hopes of reaching the port of Antwerp, combining the elements of surprise, rough ground, and bad weather for a quarter-million man offensive. On December 16, 600 tanks broke through the thinly manned American lines after a tremendous artillery barrage, creating a bulge or pocket they hoped to exploit to the sea, and sowing desperation, panic, and confusion. The weather cleared just before Christmas, and American air power helped to turn the tide as temperatures plunged to the coldest in European memory during the winter of 1944–45.

would send two photographic planes with P-51 escorts, the idea being that at least one would get back. A 'black star priority' mission might be perhaps on an oil refinery, or ball-bearing factories, sometimes a bridge. It would be varied, and actually, the pilot didn't necessarily know the specific target, but was told to take in the area, and it would include whatever they were after.

Toward the end, I was made commanding officer of the outfit of 2,500 men. The regulations required that the commanding officer of a combat squadron be a pilot, and at the age of 22, I was the oldest and most experienced pilot in the squadron!

The Last Mission

The last mission I took was on April 26 of 1945; I think that may have been the last mission of the war. My buddy Tom Vaughan from Texas also had a mission that day, and I can't remember who took off first or who landed last, but I believe that it was the last mission of the war, and a bad one at that. It was to Prague, Czechoslovakia, and when we got over there, one of the targets was an airfield. As we went over the airfield—and usually when we took pictures we were at about 25,000 feet, but going in and coming out, my personal tactic was to be much higher, as high as 39,000 feet—I looked down and I saw two fighters taking off from that airfield. The airfield had black marks on it, which meant that it was a jet field. We were terrified of these jets because they were at least a hundred miles an hour faster than we were and they could go higher. I had four fighters escorting me, and in a very short time I realized that the German jets were at our altitude! I called them out to my fighters and we all kept a very sharp lookout. In a surprisingly short time, I saw two specks in my rear view mirror at our altitude, and so I turned so that they would come in having a 'deflection shot' at me. I told the fighters to ram them, but this was not as dramatic as it sounds, because the closing speeds were over a thousand miles an hour, and to try to hit something [was next to impossible]. I called them out to my fighters and told them that when I said 'Break,' we would all turn into [the German jets]—it was very important that we convince them that we were trying to hit them, because if we didn't scare them off, they could make mincemeat out of us. What I did know was that the [German flight command on the] ground was listening to our conversations and was advising [the German pilots], and I thought that what we were saying would scare them. I counted on the fact that they knew the war was almost over, and that they were not anxious to get killed at this point, either.

It worked. We did come awfully close to them, but they only made one pass—the lead man, of course, was after me because I was the photographic plane, and he went under me. I could see him very plainly in the cockpit as he went under me, and he turned and went down, and that was the last we saw of them.

We had a range I would say of 1,200 or 1,300 miles. Fuel was always a problem coming back, but there were emergency fields in England down near the White Cliffs of Dover where we could land and refuel. Also, late in the war, there were airfields in Germany and in France. One of the times that I came back very low on fuel I ran into a thunderstorm over Holland, and I didn't know whether I was going to make it across the Channel or not. I didn't have much choice, so I went on to a field called Manston, which was a huge square paved field made especially for emergency landings; it was 10,000 feet square and so you could land in any direction and get a lot of runway. I landed there at the end of that mission. When I went to taxi in, I put the throttles forward a little bit, and both engines quit!

War's End

When the war ended, I'll tell you it was the greatest relief I've ever had in my life. I can remember that a sergeant came to me—we knew it was coming, probably a week or even more before, we just didn't know exactly when—he wanted to know if it was all right if they went out and bought some beer. I said I thought that was a wonderful idea, and so they went out and they bought six barrels. Now I'm not talking about a little 10-gallon thing, I'm talking about a barrel. Six barrels appeared and they brought them in on a 6x6 truck, and I had them put them in the ammunition dump, which was guarded 24 hours a day. The ammunition dump was also the coolest place because it was underground. When Churchill made his announcement that the war was over, we sent the trucks down there and they rolled the beer up onto the trucks and brought it to the squadron, and by the way, other squadrons had done something similar. We rolled the barrels out on top of the bomb shelter, which was elevated and could easily be tapped right there, and you never saw so many drunk guys in your life!

I didn't return home until May 26, 1946, which was about a year later. I stayed over there and I flew—I hate to admit this, but I signed up to fly for what at that point was 'Air Transport Command.' I was a multi-engine pilot, so I qualified, and frankly, the reason I did it was because I didn't want to go to the Pacific. I had had the war up to here [*gestures with hands*], and I was terrified and I was a nervous wreck. I knew that I could stay in Europe, so I signed up for a year. [Of course, when I did get home], there was a family celebration; I was met at the train by my folks, my aunt and uncle, and it was very emotional.

I went back to my college for one day. I hadn't even signed up yet, but I could get in, I knew, and I was at the dormitory and my roommate was sixteen years old! He was wet behind the ears, and I couldn't stand him in the first hour; I spent just one day there. I just knew that I would never be able to concentrate on college, so I left there and went up to Lockport, and very fortunately I got a very physical job at a cotton bleaching plant. My first job for a long time was to haul bales of cotton like a donkey from the warehouse into the plant, and that was the best thing that ever happened to me, because of course I had lots of trouble sleeping at that time. I can tell you that if you haul cotton all day, you will sleep [at night]! I stayed there for about a year and a half, and it was a wonderful transition for me. After that I got married and went to work for a box-making factory in Newark, New York, and I was near my hometown and [my life] took off from there.

I think [my experiences in World War II] made me a much better person. One of the experiences that I didn't mention was that at the end of the war, I had a mission, and I don't remember where it was to, but I was all alone and on the way back I ran low on fuel. I landed at Munich, Germany— the Munich area had just recently been [taken]; I remember the runway was all bombed out, and I had difficulty landing. They didn't have any aviation fuel, so I had to spend the night. When I got out of my plane, the first person I bumped into was Captain Cook, the [former] head of our military police at our base [near Oxford], and he had been transferred to Munich to keep order there.

He took me in his Jeep downtown to where I was going to spend the night, and by the way, my roommate that night was a Russian, so the conversation was very sparse. But Cook then took me to Dachau concentration camp and it had just been liberated. It was the most shaking experience of my life. We went in, and I can remember the first thing that struck me as we went through the gates in his Jeep was the smell; I vomited right as we went into the gate. We drove around the compound, and we had to drive very slowly because these people were in such terrible shape that they couldn't get out of the way very well. And they would come up and they would touch us on the shoulder and say 'Danke,' 'thank you.' We went to one area where they had dug a trench with a bulldozer—oh, it must have been eight feet wide and a hundred feet long—and they were pushing bodies into this common grave with a bulldozer, believe it or not. And that was a horrible experience as far as I was concerned, something I will never ever forget, very difficult.[32]

John Weeks enjoyed a long career in business and later in life settled into the communities surrounding Hometown, USA, volunteering in hospitals and medical centers and as a hospice caregiver in Washington County. He passed away on October 21, 2015, in Glens Falls, at the age of 93.

---

[32] *something I will never ever forget*-Dachau was liberated on April 29, 1945, by U.S. forces. I speculate that Mr. Weeks was there in the week that followed; it was a traumatic experience for GIs. This topic is dealt with extensively in my book *A Train Near Magdeburg*.

Richard Faulkner, World War II.

CHAPTER FOUR

The Evadee

Richard Faulkner was born on October 8, 1924, a couple hours' drive west of Hometown, USA. He graduated from high school in 1942. He became a ball turret gunner on a B-17 in the 100th Bomb Group, nicknamed 'The Bloody Hundredth' for losing many aircraft and crews. In Richard's case, he was miraculously his crew's only survivor of a mid-air collision with another B-17 of the 100th Bomb Group, only a few hours into their very first mission. He then spent twenty-nine days evading the Germans in France with the help of the French Underground, eventually being picked up by boat off the coast of France. In crossing the English Channel, his rescuers came under fire by German fast attack boats, and one of the British gunners was killed. Faulkner manned the fallen gunner's weapon, and they made it back to England.[15] 'I don't go to the reunions of my bomb group because there's hardly anybody there that I knew. I mean, I was only there nine days. I was in France longer than I was in England.'

*

Richard J. Faulkner

My father died when I was 12. I was one of five children [growing up in the Depression], and we all had to pitch in to help.

[On December 7, 1941] I was [listening to] a Chicago Bears football game when it broke in with the news about Pearl Harbor. I was surprised and I didn't even know where Pearl Harbor was.

I enlisted two days after I turned 18, in October 1942. And when I went into the service, I immediately signed up for benefits for my mother, to help her out financially. But they didn't take me until December 11, 1942.

I went into the Air Corps because I wanted to fly. I wanted to get into the pilot program, but I didn't pass it. I went to Miami Beach, spent two weeks at Miami Beach, and then to Goldsboro, North Carolina, to airplane and engines school, and spent two months there. From there I went to gunnery school in Fort Myers, Florida, for two months, and then to Dalhart Army Air Base in Texas, where I was assigned to the group training. We got ready to go overseas, and my pilot didn't pass the proficiency test. So we went to Pyote, Texas, for another month.

Then we got ready and went to Grand Island, Nebraska, and picked up our airplane, a B-17G. We flew to Grenier Field, New Hampshire, then to Goose Bay, Labrador, to Iceland, and to Stornoway, Scotland. From there we were processed, and we went to further gunnery training at the Wash in England.[33]

I was in the same crew all the way through training and flying over to England, and we were assigned to the 100th Bomb Group. We wanted to name our plane *Esquire Lady*, but we didn't last that long. We were shot down on our first mission.

---

[33] *the Wash in England-* the square bay and estuary on the east coast of England, among the largest in the UK.

Richard Faulkner and his crew, World War II.

We were going to Augsburg, Germany, and to Munich. We were in the part of the group that was assigned to Munich, and we flew the plane that was assigned to us that day, the *Berlin Playboy*.

We were delayed an hour for takeoff because of the fog. We got airborne, and soon after crossing the Channel, the plane above us got hit. And it came down and hit us, broke us into two pieces. I was in the ball turret, and I had a parachute in there; being small, I could get one in there.

The airplane broke into two parts right behind the wing. The tail part flipped over. I was with the tail, with the tail gunner and the two waist gunners. And the other part [of the B-17] had the radio man, the bombardier, navigator, pilot, and co-pilot. But they just couldn't get out, evidently, and on the other plane, there were only two people that got out. So, nine plus seven—sixteen people were killed.[34]

---

[34] *nine plus seven—sixteen people were killed-* On this mission, the 100th Bomb Group lost 3 airplanes and thirty men. This incident claimed over half

[When the tail] turned upside-down, [the ball turret where I was] was now on top. I got the door handles open—it can only open in the stowed position from the outside, and it just happened to be that way. I was just lucky it was in the position where I could open the door. I had the chute hooked on my harness, so when I got out of the turret, I hooked the rest of it on the way down.

I was in a free-fall. When I could make out objects on the ground, I pulled the ripcord. I pulled the D-ring and nothing happened. So, there are three little snaps that cover the pilot chute. I got those unsnapped, and fished the pilot chute out. And luckily it pulled out, and it pulled the rest of the parachute out. I landed in a heap by some woods on a hillside, in a pasture.

The Farmer

I gathered up my chute and carried it over into the woods, and found a bunch of leaves and berry bushes, and I hid everything in there. The goggles and the helmet, the parachute and the harness, the whole works. I saw that there was a farm nearby, so I started for there. But I could see the Germans coming. So I got back and buried myself in the berry brambles, in the leaves. And when they came through, they didn't want to look in the berry bushes, so I didn't get found out.

---

of the men and 2 out of three of the planes. The technical details are as follows for Richard's crew: Killed in Action, Munich, 18/3/44-Pilot: Paul Martin, Co-pilot: Tom Cryan, Navigator: Tom Hughes, Bombardier: Albert Racz, Flight engineer/top turret gunner: Levi Tonn, Radio Operator: Russ Longdon, Waist gunner: Lonnie Albin, Waist gunner: Veryl Lund, Tail gunner: John Howley. MIA-Ball turret gunner: Dick Faulkner (evaded capture); mid-air collision with 42-37913 (100BG); crashed Frevent, near Haudricourt, 16 miles SW of Poix, France. Missing Air Crew Report 3234. BERLIN PLAYBOY. Source: Imperial War Museum, www.americanairmuseum.com/aircraft/7212.

That was about noon, and then that evening, when it started to get dark, the farmer came, and I told him that I was an American. I couldn't speak French, he couldn't speak English. So he motioned for me to wait until the sun went down. So I waited and he came and got me after dark. My ankles and my knees were banged up, and he put me in the barn to begin with. And when he figured the Germans weren't looking for me, he took me in the house and put me in the bed, giving me some hot towels to soak my knees and ankles to get the swelling down.

But he kept motioning to me that there was something wrong. [I did not know what he meant], so somebody got the idea to get a mirror. And I could see I was all bloody—my face was all covered in dried blood; I had cut myself somehow coming out of the plane. And so they got that cleaned up, and the next day they moved me to another place, because the people got nervous. They thought that the Germans knew I was there, so they hustled me out after dark to another place. I heard later that they executed that family because the Germans were pretty sure I was there, because somehow they knew that there were ten people in the bomber, and only nine bodies [must have been found].

The French Underground

I went to another place, and I stayed there for about a week. Then they shipped me to another place, took me for another week or so, and then I was transported on the back of a motorcycle to another location, and we got a flat tire, right under a German machine gun outpost! And the Germans were up there laughing at us for having a flat tire, and I thought, 'If you only knew, fella, that this is an American down here.'

They had me in civilian clothes. And from there I went to Paris, where the [French Underground] was going to get a new picture and make up a false ID. They made it up, and it said I was a fifteen-year-old deaf-mute. We always laughed about it—the Germans were kind of slow, because there were so many deaf-mutes running around with IDs. [*Laughs*]

So I got the pictures taken, and they took me around sightseeing, Champs-Élysées and all that. And I was so scared, I thought all the Germans were watching me; all of them were walking around there, but it was probably the best thing [to be 'hiding'] right out in the open.

Leaving Paris

So when we got ready to leave, we were going to go on the subway. And there were two other fellas in the apartment with me. One was a big redhead, and the other was a Southerner from Houston, Texas.

The fellow in the Underground went down the stairs. When he got to the bottom, I started down, and the others followed suit, in the same way, in single file. I waited until [the leader] got to the corner of the street, then I came out of the building, and then I got to the corner, and then he was at another corner. But I didn't see any of the other fellows coming behind me, so I threw my hands up like, 'What do I do now?' And he motioned for me to come forward.

I ran into those two fellas much later, back home, after the Germans surrendered. The Gestapo picked them up as they came out the door, and they were held prisoner until the end of the war! But [I guess I blended in better]; I was short and dark like a Frenchman.

We got on the subway. The man in the Underground got in one door, and I got in another. When he gets off, I would get off. But I was standing right next to a colonel in the SS—he had a satchel handcuffed to his arm with a guard with a Sten gun. The train started up, and the SS colonel bumped into me. And he turned around to me and said, 'Pardonne-moi.' I thought, 'Oh, my God.' I thought I was done right then and there! [*Laughs*]

[They put me] on the train going from Paris to Morlaix [on the coastline in Brittany], where I eventually exited France. I had a magazine—if you're holding that up in front of your face like you're reading, most people don't bother you. When I got to Morlaix, they brought me to a deserted French farmhouse.

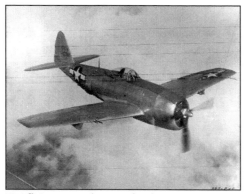

P-47N flying over the Pacific during World War II.
Credit: USAF. Public domain.

There were other people from the Underground there, and also a P-47 pilot who had been shot down. His name was Ken Williams and he had flown 63 missions. I asked him how he got shot down.

He said, 'I shot myself down. I was strafing a German bomber, and it blew up under me and blew both wings off my P-47. I ditched it, and I started running across the field. And I'm trying to hide, and I look down, and I've got the bright Mae West [life jacket] vest still on!' [*Laughs*]

Pretty soon, into the farmhouse came two ladies and two other men. One was a captain in the British intelligence, and the other fella was losing his mind, and so they tried to get him out of there before he got caught. The two ladies had just been broken out of jail. They were Underground workers, a mother and daughter. So we waited, and pretty soon they distributed some handguns to two of the Underground guys and they went out; I found out later they were to go out and watch the German machine gun [outpost]. If the Germans spotted us, they were to shoot the Germans, but if not, they were to just leave them alone, because the Underground would use the route again.

We went out and they told us to watch for the phosphorus dots in the trail and follow them—'Don't get out of the track, because it's a minefield.' So we went across the minefield, and went down the bank, down to the shore. We waited down there, and at about 4:00 in the morning they flashed a flashlight from the shore to out at sea, and the British rode in with two rubber dinghies to pick us up. They brought the pilot and me out to something like a PT boat, a British gunboat. The others were put on another one.

We were put in the hold, in the crews' quarters. We started up and got moving, and we could hear gunfire, we could hear rounds hitting the boat. The captain opened the hatch up, and he said, 'One of you guys a gunner?'

I said, 'Yes, I am.'

He says, 'Well, I just had a gunner get killed, and I need a gunner!'

I went up on top. We pulled the guy's body away and they put me on one of those .303 machine guns.[35] We kept on in the gunfight for a little while, and then two British Spitfires showed up and chased off the German E-boats. So we had quite a time out there.

Well, we got into England, and they had us put on British uniforms. When we got to London, we were issued American uniforms. I think they were trying to hide the fact [that we had been rescued] from the German [spies], but I don't think it worked.

---

[35] *.303 machine guns*-the Vickers gun, a water-cooled British machine gun with a reputation for great reliability.

I was shot down on the 18ᵗʰ day of March, 1944, and I was picked up April 16, 1944. [They had notified my mother.] I still have the telegram that my mother received. *'Regret to inform you that your son, Richard J. Faulkner, is missing on a mission over Germany.'* And no other details. My mother wrote to the adjutant general and everybody she could write to. My chaplain on the base wrote his condolences to her.

When I got back, they had a form for a telegram to send my mother. And what it said was, *'Am feeling fine, having a swell holiday.'* So she got the message [that I was okay], but that's how she found out.

*

The long anticipated D-Day invasion was imminent, and Richard was able to convey important information about the enemy.

The Underground told me that in Metz, there was a German reinforced tank battalion that could go wherever they were needed. I told [our intelligence officers] about the configuration of the minefields that we went through, and all about the machine gun posts that we saw along the road. I noted the railroad stations that had anything of importance, where the Germans had troops with guns. I told them how many I thought were in each town that I was in. But I never tried to learn the names of the people who were helping me, because if I got captured, I didn't want to have any information I could give the Germans. If I didn't know anything [about them], I couldn't tell about them.

When I got back to my group, coming back across the Channel, General LeMay—who afterwards turned out to be the head of the Air Force—[summoned] me and two other fellas who had just returned. He wanted to know what he could do to change anything, or what needed to be done, [for guys who landed in enemy territory in the future].

I said, 'Well, somebody [has just put] an order out to tie a new pair of shoes on your harness so you have a good pair of shoes [if you have to bail out]. That would never work, because the Germans would notice those new shoes right off the bat.'

He said, 'I'll rescind that, Sergeant. I'll put good <u>old</u> pair of shoes.'

But the first thing I asked General LeMay about [had to do with my mother].

I said, 'What about my allotment?' Was my mother getting her money while I was gone?

He said, 'Sergeant, I have a mother that I have an allotment for, too.'[36]

*

I had a 28-day 'survivor leave.' I went to Atlantic City, New Jersey, and they processed me there. Then they sent me to the hospital in Nashville for rehabilitation—my knees and ankles were pretty weak. And so I was there for a month, and the army sent me to B-29 school in January of '45. There were nine of us who were combat returnees, and the army wanted to send us to the Pacific, but we said we didn't want to go. By then there were a lot of other people who had never been in combat, so the army didn't make an issue of it, and they put us in a mobile training unit for airplanes and engines. And I stayed there in that unit until I got discharged on October 27, 1945.

*

I ran into the guys who were captured by the Gestapo after I left the hospital in Nashville. I was in Amarillo, Texas, and I was in the

---

[36] *General LeMay-* General Curtis LeMay (1906-1990) was one of the developers of the 'combat box' formation of the 8th Air Force over Europe, often flying with his lead crews on the most hazardous bombing missions. In the Pacific Theater, where the combat box formation style was not applicable, he became the major architect of the controversial strategic firebombing campaign, discussed in my first book, *Voices of the Pacific Theater.* He was later Chief of Staff of the United States Air Force from 1961 to 1965.

PX. [The two of them were there, recognized me, and] hollered at me. My wife always said, 'Don't rob a bank, because everybody remembers you.' [*Laughs*] And they were kidding me about [how I got away and they were captured]. They told me about how as PoWs, the Germans kept moving them as the Americans kept getting closer, that they had them march on the outside of the formation, so if anybody was going to get shot, they were it. They were getting low on food and everything, but they made it out. They got through it.

I saw the P-47 pilot, Ken Williams, after he moved to Rochester, New York, after he retired. He became a lieutenant colonel. I found his name on a list of an 'escapee-evadee' association I joined. I called him up and I went up to see him in Rochester. My wife said, 'Look at the two of you. [For escapee-evadees], you're like two midgets! You're supposed to look like John Wayne.' [*Laughs*]

I sent a letter to him a year ago, and I got no answer. So I have no idea what happened to him, whether he moved away. His wife was a teacher. I got an idea that maybe they moved when she retired.

*

My wife and I took a trip to France two years ago, and we got to Normandy, near the cemetery where my crewmates were buried. I only had about fifteen minutes, but I found three of the fellows who were in the plane with me. The other six, they sent their bodies back home, evidently. But those three, they were still there.

*

On January 14, 2014, Richard Faulkner was officially awarded his Purple Heart by his congressman in the company of his family and 100 others gathered to witness the event. In 1944, he had turned down the medal.

'I don't think you can understand. I'll always have a guilty feeling that asks, 'Why me? Why did I get out, and nobody else? Why should I still be

around, and not them?' But I have talked to other people, survivors, and they feel the same way. It makes you appreciate being alive an awful lot. I just appreciate everything; it just amazes me how lucky I was.'

Richard Faulkner passed away on August 29, 2014, at the age of 89.

CHAPTER FIVE

The P-38 Pilot

George T. FitzGibbon was born in Staten Island, New York, on October 23, 1921. He joined the U.S. Army Air Corps in January 1942, shortly after the bombing of Pearl Harbor. After graduating from flight training in October 1942, he flew the P-38 Lightning and was shot down in June 1943, parachuting into the Mediterranean. Captured and held for a short time by the Italians, he was transferred to Stalag Luft III in Poland. He was a prisoner of war for 22 months. 'The day after Pearl Harbor, I was out at the airfield applying for my cadet training, and I was accepted. I went into the Army Air Corps Program.'

*

George T. FitzGibbon

At the time of the Pearl Harbor attack, I was a student primarily trying to get enough credits so I could get into the Army Air Corps Flying Cadet Program. That was my goal all along, so I had just about completed half the credits for the degree I needed, and Pearl Harbor was attacked.

I was in a restaurant called the Hobby House in Fort Wayne, not far from where I was living at the time. It was about 1:00 in the afternoon, and I was having a nice big hamburger. It was announced over the speaker system in the restaurant that Pearl Harbor was attacked. My first question was, 'Where is Pearl Harbor?' A Navy guy lived in our house, so he enlightened me as to Pearl Harbor. Boy, we got talking about this fast. 'Boy, this is going to be serious business.' Anyway, I used it as a catalyst to get into my flying program. Flying just always appealed to me since I was like 15 or so. I didn't have any experience other than riding in the backseat of a little open cockpit plane a couple times. I read a lot about it and thought that was what I wanted to do. This just provided the means for me to do it.

I went down to Maxwell Air Force Base in Alabama. Then after the basic training there, I went to primary flying school at Decatur, Alabama, [to learn with] a PT-17, a Stearman biplane. Then I went to Greenville, Mississippi, for basic training. That was the Vultee BT-13. Then back to Selma, Alabama, for advanced, a North American AT-6. The last 10 hours were in a World War II fighter. They had three different types. They had a P-36, a P-39, and a P-40. You drew to see which one you were going to get, and I drew the old P-36. Anyway, I flew my last 10 hours of flying school in a P-36, [but] it was the most sophisticated thing I'd flown so far, so I thought a lot of it. It wasn't as good as a P-40, I don't think, but I got 10 hours in it, and it helped me a lot. Then I graduated and proceeded from there.

I was assigned to Pinellas County Airport down in Florida, where we had P-40s, and I flew the P-40 down there for a couple of months. I was commissioned as a 2nd lieutenant, and then got shipping instructions to New York City and then a boat over to England. We went on the *Queen Elizabeth*, unescorted except for the first 500 miles. They went fast, and they changed course every three minutes. That was their evasive action, I guess, and we didn't have any problem. It was a rough-weather trip, but it took five days. We ended up in Glasgow, Scotland. We were assigned to a little base and airfield up there in Northern England called Shaftesbury. That was about the 24th of November of '42.

The trouble with Shaftesbury is it was a nice little military base, but it didn't have an airfield. We were about a dozen replacement pilots. They also didn't have any P-40s in England, which we were all prepared in, so we hung around there and played cards and went down to the pubs and things like this for a couple months until they asked. They wanted five volunteers to go down to North Africa. That was all they could tell us about it, it was down in North Africa, so I volunteered. I sailed in a convoy this time, and I think one of our ships got torpedoed. We saw the smoke, but that was about all I could tell. We came in through the Strait of Gibraltar, a nice calm Mediterranean Sea. I said, 'Oh, what a heavenly place for submarines.' [Laughs] We didn't have any problem.

We went into Oran, stayed overnight there, and then we went to a little pasture-type airfield about 20 miles out of Casablanca called Berrechid, Morocco. We had a couple old trainers there that we flew for a while. Then we found out they were bringing P-38s into Casablanca by ship, partially disassembled, but they'd reassemble them right there in Casablanca Airport. About five of us finagled getting checked out in the P-38; they used us to fly airplanes up to the front, after they were assembled. We did that for four or five trips, then we got orders to stay up there and join the 82nd Fighter Group.

P-38J flying over Southern California. Credit: USAF. Public domain.

The P-38 was wonderful, a dream machine. The only disadvantage was it was slow to roll. If you wanted to roll into a steep turn or steep bank to evade the enemy for instance, it took a little more time to get into that position than you wanted it to. With a single-engine fighter, you just hit that stick right over there and whip it right up. Anyway, it never adversely affected me.

Combat

Then I was assigned to the 96th Fighter Squadron flying missions right away out of Telerghma in North Africa. We'd go out over the Mediterranean, sometimes escorting bombers to Sardinia and Sicily; sometimes we'd go out on a shipping sweep. You could attack any ships you saw on the Mediterranean, because you didn't have to worry about identifying the enemy—anything you see out there is the enemy. We'd strafe boats and ships and drop bombs on them. I'd go down when I'd strafed a ship, and it looked like all those tracers are coming right between your eyes. We carried one 500-pound bomb on one side and a fuel tank on the other side, for equalization. The trouble was, you couldn't release one. You couldn't drop your empty fuel tank without dropping the bomb, too, so you'd keep them both until you got ready to drop the bomb and then punch the button. I don't think we ever did much damage with a bomb—we didn't have a bombsight. You just dive down and hope you're somewhere in the ballpark.

Following the Axis defeat in North Africa, the Allies pursued them to the island of Sicily. On July 10, 1943, U.S. and British forces began Operation Husky, an invasion of the island using troops deployed by gliders, parachutes, and landing craft.

When we got around Sicily, especially, we ran into a lot of fighters, Italian fighters and Focke-Wulf 190s, German fighters. I shot down a Macchi 202 Italian fighter that I got credit for. The day we invaded Sicily, enemy fighters were flying down to the southern tip of Sicily and strafing our troops. Then they'd go back to refuel, so we were on them when they came back to take on more fuel.

An Italian Macchi C.202 fighter at Wright-Patterson Field outside Dayton, Ohio, for United States Army Air Forces evaluation.
Credit: USAF. Public domain.

I was on my 25th mission and we got involved in a big dogfight there. I had a Focke-Wulf 190 in my sights, and I was shooting at him with everything I had—parts of him were just coming off. Just then something hit me in my left engine, and it was on fire. Black smoke just poured in through the wing root, right up into the cockpit, and all of a sudden, I couldn't see a thing, just the sky straight up. My little world was coming to an end.

A captured Focke-Wulf Fw 190A. Credit: USAF. Public domain.

I don't know [if it was part of his airplane that hit me]; I've been trying to figure that out for years. Possibly it was [another] fighter, but we were only about 200 feet off the ground, and I thought that I saw fire coming from places on the ground. We checked this out after the war, and nobody in Western Sicily reported shooting down a P-38 that day. I think it was ground fire. Anyway, it didn't make much difference. The smoke [was too much]; there was nothing I could do but get out of the plane. I pulled it up and released the canopy and unhooked my seatbelt and rolled it over. I pushed on the wheel and I fell out.

Now I'd say I was at about 800 feet. I was wearing a seat pack, and the seat pack caught on the canopy hinge back there, so I was hanging there out of the airplane. I couldn't do anything except kick my feet a little bit, and pretty soon it broke loose. Then I watched the airplane go by, and I pulled the ripcord. I pulled it and nothing happened. I pulled it again a little harder. Sure enough, that did it, so I landed in the Mediterranean Sea about 200 yards offshore.

Captured

I hit the water fast. When I was coming down, I didn't have much altitude to lose. You're supposed to get yourself undone out of this harness before you get in the water if you can; [I couldn't get out of it completely].Then the parachute fell over, and I was able to get my hand onto that, and I got it undone. I had a rubber boat in my seat pack and I had a Mae West life jacket on, but the water was only up to here [*gestures chest-high with hand*], and I was 200 yards offshore. I stood on the bottom and looked inshore. There's these three guys in there that were waving me to come in, so they fired a couple of shots on each side of me to get my attention, I guess. Anyway, I walked in. It was like a spit out there, because as I walked in, it got deeper, and then the bottom came back up again. I had a .45 sidearm right here [*gestures under left arm*], and didn't know what I was going to do with that, so I took it out and laid it on the bottom of the Mediterranean Sea, and I walked in. The guy says, 'For you, the war is over.' He was pretty near right, even though there was a lot of war left yet.

These were Italian soldiers. We walked to the village of Castelvetrano and went to a place that I think was an officers' club. It was like 7:00 in the evening. The place was loaded and they all had drinks in their hand. I guess the commanding officer was the guy they took me to. [Other than that], there was no conversation or anything. He gave the guy some instructions, and they took me down the street and put me up on the second floor of this little building, right in the middle of the village, and left the guard there with me. About an hour later, a guy came with a dinner for me, a nice piece of Salisbury steak, some spinach, and maybe a little spaghetti and some wine in the bottle. I said if I'd known the food was going to be this good, I could have come sooner, because we were eating C-rations where we came from. [*Laughs*] I stayed there about a couple of nights, I guess, and then I was loaded on a bus, and we drove up to Palermo. There were five guards and me and we stayed right in the airport operations building, Palermo Airport, second floor, with one guard with me all the time.

That night, I had to go to the restroom. The guard was sitting there on the bed, leaning on his rifle. He's dozing like this [*mimics drowsiness/sleep*]. I indicated that I was going to the restroom. All the window openings had no glass or anything like that. I jumped out of a window onto a landing, and I took off around two o'clock in the morning. He didn't hear me or anything—nobody saw me, so I walked west for half a mile or so. I went up through the city and there were no people around—everybody was asleep, I guess. I walked maybe three miles or so; now I was starting to think it's going to get light pretty quick and I'd better find a place to situate myself during the daytime.

Before I could decide on exactly what to do, I walked right into an Italian gun position. They were covering the road coming up from the south, with this big gun up on the top. First thing I knew, I hear this sound of metal clicking, and this big searchlight comes on. I put my hands up. I was right in the light, so I was recaptured again. Fortunately, they didn't shoot. They sure had the drop on me that time, though I was so close to General Patton's army, which would be coming through there in just two or three days' time. While Montgomery went up the east coast, Patton came around the other way, but I was back to being a PoW again.

The Allied 'finish line' in the battle for Sicily was Messina, which fell to General Patton's army in a spectacular conclusion in mid-August 1943. Unfortunately, more than 100,000 Axis forces escaped to mainland Italy across the Straits of Messina, taking Allied prisoners with them by boat.

Then we were put on a bus and taken to Messina. Messina had just been attacked, [but had not yet fallen]; they were still in the war there in Messina. There were a couple of civilian bodies lying right out on the street, not military; I don't remember if we could hear the guns there or not. There were now about five or six of us, all American pilots like me, and the Italians loaded us in a launch and took us across the Straits of Messina right in the middle of the day. I was worried we were going to get strafed out in the middle of the straits, but we made it across.

*

We walked. You do a lot of walking as a PoW. We got to a railroad, and they loaded us in a couple of boxcars. By now, there were 66 of us; they put 33 of us in each boxcar, and we took off.

We got up to the south of Salerno. The Salerno marshalling yards were all bombed out, so they pulled [the railcars] off on a siding and unhooked the engine, and the Italians went their own way. The guards just sat out there and laughed and had a big time talking. They had their own provisions. Nobody seemed to be putting any effort into getting us something to eat. We sat there for seven days, I think. The fourth day, they came around with a big kettle of some kind of brothy soup. It wasn't very good, but it tasted like heaven at the time. Then the Germans evidently heard that we were there, and they came down with three lorries and loaded us all on those three trucks and drove us around Salerno to a place called Capua, just northeast of Naples. It was a barbed wire camp, and we stayed in there a week or two. Now they're getting the prisoners all together. They must have had several hundred by then. Funny thing, only about a quarter of a mile from us was this brick factory, sitting right out in the open. It turned out to be a small arms factory. One day the B-25s came over and bombed that thing—that was exciting. It blew up for like 12 hours, boxcars and all. You just kept hearing one big blast. We'd say, 'Well, that's it for now.' Then another one!

Boy, it lasted a long time. They had masonry ceilings in our buildings, and the masonry came down and cut up a lot of guys.

We were prisoners of the Italians for like three months. We left that camp and got up to a place called Sulmona, which is east of Rome, in what had been a civilian prison. It had big 15-foot masonry walls, and it made thoughts of escape very difficult. Italian guards would be walking the top of that wall, until one day in September, they were gone, and the German paratroopers were up there. That's how we found out that Italy had capitulated.

On July 25, 1943, Benito Mussolini was dismissed as prime minister by the Fascist Grand Council. King Victor Emmanuel III had him arrested and then appointed the 'Hero of Ethiopia,' Marshal Pietro Badoglio, who promptly signed an armistice with the Allies on September 3. A furious Hitler disarmed the Italian army fighting with the Germans and sent 600,000 into slave labor.[16] Mussolini, being held at a mountaintop resort, was later rescued in a daring SS glider raid ten days after Italy broke from Germany. The German war machine now poured into Italy and dug in.

A couple weeks later, the Germans marched us down to the railroad and got us loaded in the boxcars, and we went up north. We had several stops along the route. They'd just stop for a couple hours, right out in the open, but they wouldn't let us out of the cars. Finally, we got into Bolzano, up in the Alps, right at the southern end of the Brenner Pass, at about 10 minutes to noon. We could hear our bombers almost before the train stopped. At the 12:00 bombing time, it turned out their targets were this railroad bridge and the [marshalling] yards right at the southern end of Bolzano! Somebody ran up and down and opened all the boxcars; the PoWs did this, not the Germans. You have a choice you have to make. Everybody is running like crazy. Do I go right or left? It scared the heck out of all of us.

I went left into the city of Bolzano. If I had gone right, there were some open lots out there, and then the river was out there, so I might have had a better chance to escape if I'd gone to the river because I can swim good. Anyway, I went left with another fella with me. People were all in the bomb shelters, so there was nobody out, except a German guard here and there to try to keep us contained a little bit. We saw this guard down the middle of the street, so we zipped into a building. We went up the stairs; everybody else was in the basement. We got to the top and went over another building, and we came down on the far side of this guard. Then we walked up the street, maybe a half a mile, right in the city. The third wave of bombers had already come over, and people were now coming out of the shelters, and the streets were getting full of people. We said, 'What are we going to do now?' We look like Americans right off the bat, you know, so we'll have to pull into one of these estate-like places, like a one-acre property with a lot of hedges and shrubs around. We pulled into one, got in behind the hedges, and we're sitting there, figuring we'll wait until dark and then get out of there. A German guy comes out with a Luger, and he says, 'Komm her,' so somebody had seen us going in there. We were recaptured and returned back to the rest of the troops.

We went back on the same train, went up north through the Brenner Pass, up to Munich. From there, we walked up to Moosburg, a big barbed wire camp. Later, towards the end of the war, we were back in Moosburg again, and there were like 30,000 of us in there. Anyway, we got in there, and we stayed there a couple of weeks.

Then we went back on the train again, and we went up north. We went all the way to Sagan, I guess. That's about 90 kilometers southeast of Berlin on the Oder River. That was where Stalag Luft III was, and we moved into there.

We stayed there for a year and a half. That's where *The Great Escape* [movie took place], and [that compound] was just over the fence. We couldn't see any of this, and we didn't even know it was going on. We had tunnel projects of our own. In fact, we had three going on in our barracks. It was Barracks 55, and we were in a corner, fairly close to the fences, but you had to tunnel a long ways. It was all sandy ground. That's where all our bed slats went, to holding up the sand [tunnels] from collapsing.

We developed a system after a while. The Germans would know that you had tunneling going on. They'd wait a while, and then they'd come in all of a sudden and search for the tunnel. We had two tunnels that we called 'diversionary tunnels.' They were the ones that were supposed to be found by the Germans. Then the other one was the main event, and hopefully they wouldn't find that one, but they did in our case. Eventually, they found it, but it gave us something to do.

[To conceal it], we had a stove. It was the same way as it was in Stalag 17. Did you ever see that in the movie? They had a stove, a little potbelly stove. We did a little carpenter work under it, and we made it so the stove would sit there, but you could take the whole thing down in a flash and move the stove over and pull the whole panel up. Then you go down about 10 feet, and there's your tunnel. Anyway, it kept everybody busy. If you did nothing else, you had to carry sand around in your pockets and unload the sand somewhere. We used to dump it around shrubs and stuff like that, but the sand was real white. The surface sand was brown, so it was hard to conceal. The Germans knew we were doing it all the time. Eventually, we just went into the outhouse and dumped the sand right down the holes.

We played a lot of bridge; played bridge all winter and played softball all summer. And if it wasn't for the Red Cross, we'd have been in dire straits. The Germans would give a bowl of soup on

Thursday. Maybe you'd get a potato or two per person for the rest of the week. You never could tell what day you were going to get it. Every six weeks, they'd give you a piece of the reddest, most luscious-looking steak you ever saw, but it was horsemeat. It was so tough you could hardly eat it. You could take a little bite of that, and you could chew it for an hour, which we did. Anyway, the Red Cross parcels, you're supposed to get one per person a week. We were getting about one parcel for six or seven guys there for the first year or so, but then as the war started winding down a little bit, after we were on the continent, things started picking up a little bit. I think the Germans started getting worried about who was going to get blamed for mistreatment, and stuff like that. The camp commander wasn't any dummy. He was going to protect his ends, so we ended up getting one parcel for four people the last few months, so that was good. There was some sugar and a can of either Spam or something like that, cocoa. Our cooks made some great things.

Oh, we did get bread. That's the main thing the Germans gave us was bread, like a pumpernickel loaf. It was not big, and it was black. We [heard] that the sawdust content was reduced to 10%, so I don't know what it was before that. Anyway, you could cut a slice of that about an eighth of an inch thick, and hold it right on the edge; it wouldn't even bend. [*Laughs*] Good stuff. I was a great bread eater all my life, and it was great. We'd get one-eleventh of a loaf of bread per day, per person. For breakfast, you'd have a piece of bread with some margarine on it. You'd get margarine in the Red Cross parcels. The Red Cross really saved us.

The guards were older. Most of them had been on the Russian front. They'd been wounded, and some of them were a little bit crippled from their wounds, a limp or an arm that they couldn't straighten out or something like that, and all [seemed to be] older guys. Yeah, we got along well with them. We didn't do anything to antagonize them. They were just hoping the war would be over soon, same as we were.

They had speakers in the camp, and we'd get German news broadcasts every afternoon. That was slanted, of course, and you didn't always get the truth from them. I remember when Cassino fell. It took them about four days to admit on the German broadcast that the Battle of Cassino... They never did say they lost it, but they say, 'We moved back to better defensive positions during the night,' or something like this.[37] Some ingenious Englishman there built some kind of radio that he could get the BBC broadcasts from. He kept it hidden. Nobody knew where it was, and nobody in our camp knew where it was. He copied that down every morning and sent it out on a piece of paper to somebody who was authorized to travel from one compound to another. They'd come in. The guy would come in with his piece of paper, and he'd brief everybody in the barracks on it after we posted guards to make sure that no Germans were around, so we'd get the BBC within 24 hours. We knew when the [D-Day] invasion occurred, and we heard all the high points: Saint-Lô and Caen and all those.

*

My mother received notification that I was a PoW about two to three months after I was captured, but my brother was in the 1st Armored Division. He came through our area there in North Africa when they were going back to rest camp after Tunisia fell. He met some of the guys in my squadron. Lo and behold, later he ran into

---

[37] *Battle of Cassino*-The Allies waged a months-long struggle in the first half of 1944 to dislodge Germans entrenched at a centuries-old monastery in the mountains on their way to Rome. At the time it was considered a paramount objective, and the Benedictine abbey was reduced to rubble by American heavy bombers—which ironically gave German paratroopers greater flexibility and cover in its defense. Monte Cassino fell on May 19, 1944, after over 50,000 Allied casualties and 20,000 Germans killed or wounded.

one of the same guys, probably at rest camp, too. This guy told my brother that I had been shot down, but they told him I bailed out, and they thought I was all right, so he wrote my mother. Everything was pretty good until she got that telegram.

My mother could write to me. I don't think she was restricted on how often she could write to me, but she was restricted on things she could send me. She could send a little box about every 60 days. I'd write about once a week to her, once a week to my girlfriend. After we got communicating, which took like six months of back and forth before we got our records straight, then she was sending me long winter underwear and socks. The box would be opened, and I'd go through everything. As far as I know, everything was there. I ended up with two sets of long winter underwear. When we marched out of that camp, I had both sets on. It was January 1945, and there was six inches of snow.

Marched Out

We marched south. I can't remember the little villages we passed through, but our terminal was a town called Cottbus.[38] It was about 45 or 50 miles, and it took us five days to get there because there were 10,000 of us. The winter conditions didn't help any. The first night out was absolutely wicked. You're all spread out, 10,000 guys. Some guys probably had good accommodations, relatively. Our group ended up in a stable. We slept on a concrete floor of this stable that didn't have any windows in it or doors. The wind whistled through there. We each had one blanket. This fellow from Wisconsin and I bunked together, so it gave us one blanket below and one above. It was a miserable night. Then we were out walking again the whole next day. We ended up in a factory, the second

---

[38] Cottbus is the second-largest city in Brandenburg, Germany, about 125 km southeast of Berlin, and a major railway junction.

floor of a factory.[39] The heat was pouring up in that place so much you could hardly... What a contrast, you know? It almost drove us right out it was so hot, one extreme to another.

Colonel Spivey was our camp commander, quite a wonderful gentleman. I'm sure he did a lot of things that I wasn't aware of, but he also did a lot of things that we all weren't aware of. I can't think of anything specific right now, but he was protecting us all the time and fighting with the German kommandant. There again, the story went that he got easier to fight with as the war progressed. Anyway, then we got on the train at Cottbus and took off, and we got in Leipzig just before midnight. Sure enough, we just got in there, and the air raid sirens went off, but we didn't have to wait too long, and they pulled the train out. What did happen was 10,000 guys had just had this soup, or some damn thing that the Germans served us and called it soup. We didn't know what was in it, and we hadn't had any solid food to speak of. I had a little bit of bread and margarine and cheese, but I was rationing that to myself, so we were all very hungry, and we ate this soup.

We got in Leipzig, and everybody needed to go to the bathroom. They opened up the doors. I think there were like 2,000 in our group on this train. We took one look around. There were women and kids. There are no men, just the guards. One of the sights of the war was watching 2,000 men go to the bathroom right out there in the open, I guess, with all these people watching. We had no choice.[40]

---

[39] *We ended up in a factory*-this march is further discussed in the chapter entitled 'B-17 PoW Reunion'; they were evacuated away from the rapidly advancing Russian armies. The factory refers to a pottery factory, and the fact that these freezing, sick prisoners were given shelter there saved many lives on the evacuation march.

[40] *We had no choice*-the men were probably suffering extreme intestinal discomfort due to the contaminated 'soup.' This incident is also recounted in the chapter entitled 'B-17 PoW Reunion.'

We got out of Leipzig and went down to Munich. Then we walked back up to Moosburg, and we spent the rest of the war there. There were 30,000 prisoners there then. A lot of them were Hungarians and Greeks and Romanians, people from that part of Europe. I know we had some civilians in there. Anyway, we were separated a little bit from them, not completely.

Liberation

We'd walk around for exercise. I got to be a good walker. That's what I did in Stalag III, I'd walk around that compound I don't know how many times. It's a thousand yards around, and I'd get my legs in shape. That really helped me when we marched out of there, I can tell you that. So I was walking around with a friend one morning. I think it was the 28th of April, and we could look up there on the hill. We could see something coming out of the woods, and we didn't know what the heck it was. It turned out to be a Sherman tank!

We got it on the radio that General Patton's army had got to Nuremberg, and elements of his army had turned south. That's what they said, so sure enough, here comes some of his army. Pretty soon, there were six tanks up there. Then the small arms fire started right in the woods, right next to us. We didn't even know there was anybody out there, and all this machine gun fire was starting up! We all piled into the trench we had and tried to watch the war [in front of us].

The village of Moosburg had a couple of church steeples, and the Hitler Youth went up in the church steeples with machine guns. They were shooting up the road, so the tanks blew those churches right down, both of them.

[The guards] were exiting. I think a couple of guards got hit by gunfire, but all the rest of them were gone, and we never saw another German. This all started about 9:30 in the morning, and at 12:30, a Sherman tank came rolling right into the camp. It got a tremendous welcome. Then they put our own military police around the place so people couldn't get out, which was reasonable. We don't want to turn 30,000 people out in the roads right behind the front that had just barely gone through.

This guy, Red Hanson from Iowa, he says, 'Let's get out of here.' I said, 'I'm with you.'

We went out under the fence that night with our own guards on the fences—figured that if they saw us, they wouldn't shoot. Anyway, nobody saw us. It was pretty slim guarding, I guess, so we got out. We go down on the road, and it took us two days to get to Nuremberg. It was probably about 100 miles or so. We hitchhiked with American Jeeps and stuff, anybody who happened to be going along. Every time we got [a lift], we'd have to prove ourselves. We looked like hell, you know. I had an Eisenhower jacket on and British woolen pants and some kind of English woolen hat, a military hat, no rank insignia, nothing whatsoever, no dog tags. They were all gone. None, nothing, absolutely nothing. The first guy who stopped had his pistol right out. He was a captain. We were really sad-looking, so he asked us a lot of questions about Brooklyn Dodgers and all this. Finally, we convince him we're Americans, and he gave us a ride up the road. Then we had to go through it all again; it took us two days to get to Nuremberg. We went to the wrong airfield first, but then got to the right airfield where there were C-47s bringing 50-gallon drums of gasoline in for the tanks, and we convinced the operations officer that we were Americans, even though we looked like bums. He gave us a tent to sleep in. We got on that C-47 the next day, and we flew back to Le Havre [France], and we were met there by some Red Cross ladies, who hugged us even though we looked so bad.

We went to Camp Lucky Strike. We were either among the first to go through there, or there was a lull in operations, because they had a thousand pyramid tents out there, and there were only about a half a dozen occupied.[41] We showered. Man, that was great; something as simple as a shower is awful good when you don't have any. Then they deloused us—a guy came around with what looked like a flamethrower on his back and a big hose. Boy, he blew us in places we didn't even know we had! [*Laughs*] Then they issued us new clothes. They put us on five meals a day but with restricted quantities, which was okay, because we probably would have ruptured ourselves if we'd got into all of the mashed potatoes and gravy and stuff. That worked out good.

I was only there about three days and they announced they had some openings on one of the ships going back in a 26-ship convoy to Boston, so I got on a troop ship. Actually, all the ships went to New York, but my ship went to Boston. I can't remember the name of it, but I remember we weren't on a restricted five meals a day [regimen] anymore. Boy, did I eat! [*Laughs*] I think I gained 20 pounds on that trip.

[At Boston] we got on a train and went out to Fort Devens and stayed overnight, and the next morning we were on a train again and went down to New York City, then out to Fort Dix, where I was processed out. I wasn't forced out. I had a choice. I could stay in if I wanted to, but I elected to get out, not knowing any better. I

---

[41] *Camp Lucky Strike*- The so-called 'Cigarette Camps' were located in the Le Havre, France, port area, set up immediately after the liberation of this area following D-Day as depots and supply camps for combat staging. Mr. FitzGibbon arrived as they were transitioning over to repatriating American GIs and PoWs. Camp Lucky Strike was probably the largest of these, a tent city that reached nearly 60,000 at its peak. Other camps included Old Gold, Chesterfield, Pall Mall, and five others. The code names were designated primarily for security reasons. See www.skylighters.org/special/cigcamps for a good discussion.

got out and got transportation back into Manhattan, where my mother was living at that time. My train pulled into Penn Station, evidently before my mother could get everyone there. I headed for the nearest barbershop, where I had a shampoo, a shave, and a haircut. She had my old foot locker there with all my old uniform clothes in it, so I had everything except the tie, so I got all my uniform on except the tie. Soon she arrived, followed by my Aunt Lil and Uncle Fred and Bob and Shirley, who are my cousins. We had a big rendezvous with the family and walked down to this big restaurant in Greenwich Village and had dinner. I was treated like a hero. For George FitzGibbon, the war was over.

As a reserve officer, George FitzGibbon was recalled during the Korean War when they needed pilots. He stayed in the Air Force, retiring in 1969 as a lieutenant colonel, the operations officer of the 41st Air Refueling Squadron at Griffiss Air Force base in New York. He passed away at the age of 93 on May 5, 2015.

Charlie Corea (center) and GI buddies, World War II.
Photo: Corea family.

CHAPTER SIX

The First Engineer

Charles P. Corea hailed from Rochester, New York, just north of where I went to college before returning to Hometown, USA to begin my teaching career. I did not actually have the opportunity to know him personally, but felt he shared a kinship with many profiled in this book, especially since he served in the 100th Bomb Group, 'affectionately' known by its members as 'The Bloody Hundredth.' He was trained as a flight engineer on a B-17 but did double duty as the top turret gunner on some of his missions, including his final one the day he was shot down. This interview took place just seven weeks after the September 11, 2001, terrorist attacks.

'We're all in the same boat. We all did what we had to do. I was telling this to a friend of mine the other day, that when we entered the service back in 1942, right after Pearl Harbor, all my friends and buddies and classmates, we went in and there was no doubt about what we had to do. I've never seen that much cooperation and patriotism until September 11th. That's the only good thing that came out of September 11th, the country coming together like it did back in 1941.'

*

Charles P. Corea

My godfather owned the creamery in Macedon, and my father was a cheese maker, and that's how I happened to be born in Macedon, New York. He came to this country back in the late 1800s, 1898 or 1901, and I was born there in 1921, and at the age of 18 months, we moved to East Rochester, where he worked for the dairy there. And that's how I became an 'East Rochesterian,' and I've been there ever since. Grew up in East Rochester, married the police chief's daughter—he gave me an offer I couldn't refuse, [*Laughs*] one of those things, and we've been living in the same house she was born in since then.

I graduated from East Rochester High School in 1940. For a short time I worked in the Merchant's Dispatch Transportation Company, making box cars and rail cars.

I was living with my mother and dad, and Pearl Harbor was on a Sunday. East Rochester on Friday and Saturday nights was a busy town. It was a working man's town. I used to do a little work for this fella who ran the hotel, like a gopher for the guys that played a little poker, so I generally got up a little later on Sunday morning. I remember getting up. I don't know what time of the day it was. I heard it on the news that Pearl Harbor had been bombed. Being a youngster, that was not as serious, in my estimation, as the recent happenings of 9/11 were, because the implications actually seemed a lot less to me as a person at the time. [But] the war had begun.

I remember playing cards that evening, and there were a couple of guys [who were anxious] to sign up. We were the first ones there at the draft office about 6:30 the next morning. I got called up in September of '42.

'Colorblind as a Bat'

We went to Fort Niagara and we took some aptitude tests. At the time I was gung-ho, I thought maybe I'd get into the [Air Force] cadets. I'm a young kid, I thought maybe I'd get one of those P-40s and play around with it, right? When you're young, you think you can do anything. I took a written test and passed that okay. Then I had to take a physical. At the time Fort Niagara was busier than heck. I took my eye test, passed that okay, and I was walking out the door and the guy called me back and says, 'One more test.'

That test was for color vision. He said, 'What did you see? See any numbers there?'

I kept wincing and stuff and he kept flicking the pages over. He put me down, 'Failed.' He said, 'You're colorblind as a bat!' He threw me out.

I got back [to the barracks] and the major said, 'Why'd you take the test if you knew you were colorblind?'

I said, 'I'm not colorblind. That guy was [too busy] and pushed me through like crazy.'

He picked up a yellow pencil and says, 'What color is that pencil?'

I says, 'Yellow.'

'You want to take the test over again?'

I said, 'Sure.'

The next day I got shipped out to Atlantic City. That was the end of my second test, but it turns out I am colorblind, browns and greens and stuff like that. Yellow, blues, and solid colors I can get away with.

I ended up in Atlantic City and I was with a couple of friends of mine. We stayed together, we all went in together. I remember we passed an aptitude test on whether you were a good candidate for radio or armament or photography. Having a decent education I had my choice of about seven or eight different qualifications. I remember talking to my buddy, who wanted to go to radio school, into switching over to go to photography school. I said, 'That way we'll get to do photography and we'll still get to fly around taking pictures instead of something else.' I talked him into that and he switched his number one choice from radio to photography. When I made my first choice, photography, the guy asked me, 'What do you want for a second choice?'

I said, 'I don't care.' We put down aircraft mechanics.

Well, the next call up was for aircraft mechanics, and I went and said, 'Hey, Jerry, why aren't you packing?'

He says, 'I wasn't called up.' The irony was that he ended up going to Denver to become the photographer! I ended up going down to Seymour Johnson Field in North Carolina, helping build that airfield because it was new in the war. I ended up being a mechanic for that duration they taught us. Then when we finished that particular school, they asked us, 'Who wants to take some examination for aerial gunnery?'

I says, 'I do, but I'm colorblind.'

He says, 'Go down and take it anyway.' They needed gunners pretty badly, and I passed that; instead of 20/20 I was 20/15, and he was very easy on me when I started going through the chart: 'Take your time, read the chart.' I ended up only missing four or five out of twenty. He passed me okay.

We became aerial gunners. We went down to Fort Myers, Florida, and went to school there and did some practice flying and shooting at targets. Then they took us from there and sent us to Lambert Field in St. Louis. It was at the Curtiss-Wright [plant]; they put us in that technical school. There were only 30 or 40 of us, and we had civilian instructors and they really taught us like you were going to a legitimate [military] school, the aerodynamics and the systems and the whole thing. We were the only Army personnel in the school. I got corporal stripes at Fort Myers gunnery school, and after getting out of that St. Louis school, they gave me sergeant stripes.

*

The war in Europe was going badly for bombers and they needed the B-17s. Everybody that had any knowledge of gunnery and stuff, they put them on B-17s. We went to Salt Lake City to get put on crews. Because of my training, they made me first engineer on a B-17. I had been carrying around this big technical book all the time about hydraulic systems [from the previous school], and I get on B-17 and it's all electrical. They gave me an assistant engineer who didn't know as much as I did, you know what I mean? But they needed personnel, they needed numbers.

They sent me up to Moses Lake, Washington. We trained there for quite a while forming groups: pilots, copilots, navigators and bombardiers, and the rest of the crew, which was ten people. We did some high-altitude missions and some hedge hopping. It was a fun time, because now we're flying, we're going down the Columbia River Basin, hedge hopping along the river and over the bridges and stuff like that. Here you are, twenty-one years old, and you've got the world pretty good. We'd go to places like Wenatchee, which only had about 50,000 people; we were the only Air Force personnel there. We couldn't buy anything; the people would just go to the bar, they would buy you a drink, or you'd go to the restaurant and they'd pay for the lunches. That was about the time that the Philippines was lost, and I don't know if you remember [a hero from that period] in history, Colin Kelly. Colin Kelly dove his B-17 into a Japanese destroyer, got the Congressional Medal of Honor for killing himself, and now the people were all gung-ho.[42] It's just like the euphoria that we have now with the September 11th deal.

---

[42] *Colin Kelly*-Colin Kelly, Jr. (1915-1941) piloted bombing runs against the Japanese navy in the first days after the Pearl Harbor attack. He ordered his crew to bail out during an attack shortly before his bomber exploded on

We trained and trained and trained, and now we're ready to ship out. We've got this group formed, overseas training group formed, and the next thing you know I've got to take another physical. I go in and everything's the same, and, boom, this time they give me a color test with yarn. They have different colored yarns. Well, Christ's sake, dark green, light green, brown, just flunked me again. They grounded me!

I'm saying to them, 'Hey, I've got all this training. Why the heck do I need [to see] colors? I'm going to be in a plane; all I'm going to do is shoot some [colored] flares.' Anyway, this buddy of mine got grounded because he had to go home; his wife had an emergency operation, so he lost his crew. We were chumming around before we got placed in another group, because he was a first engineer too.

He says to me, 'Go in and tell them that you were in the sunlight and the light bothered you and ask them for another test.' When they called me in for another test, he went in and took it for me.

I went in and I remember Major Barry put a waiver on my records, waived the color vision. Ray keeps telling me he took the test for me; [later] he wrote a letter about doing this for me. Anyway, to make the story chronological, I got on the crew. First thing you know, we did our training, we were flying overseas in January of '44.

Going Overseas

We had a real pilot. He was a very quiet type of guy. He never said much of anything. The copilot and the bombardier and myself, being up in front all the time, we got closer together than I did with

---

December 10, 1941, killing him. It was the first American B-17 to be shot down in combat. He was posthumously awarded the Distinguished Service Cross, and a Liberty ship was named after him.

the rest of the crew. When we got to England, we would chum around together.

I had to do a lot of jobs as the engineer. In normal duties, I logged everything. I logged the pilots, copilots, the names, the time, and all the crew. I put everything in a log: when we took off, and all the pertinent things. [I also did odd things], like during combat I remember a couple of times I had the tail-wheel pin sheared off. I had to crawl back in there and put a screwdriver in there so it would stay straight when we landed. A couple of times you had to turn the landing wheels manually to put them down; sometimes you get a little jam up in there or something like that. That was my job. In combat, I was also the top turret gunner.

We went to a place called Thorpe Abbotts.[43] It's about 99 miles north of London. It was great, but I wasn't there long enough to really enjoy it. What happened is we got there in January, but after our training we didn't get to the group until February, and they put us right into the thick of things. Everything went along pretty good until you got shot, until you went down, or until you got killed. The 'Bloody Hundredth' is probably one of your more famous groups; we ended up with [very high] casualties.

The Fifth Mission

I was shot down on March 6, just my fifth mission. It was the first daylight raid where the whole 8th Air Force got to Berlin. We tried to get there a day or two earlier and we had to abort because of bad weather conditions. A couple of wings did a couple of 180s

---

[43] *Thorpe Abbotts*- Home of the 'Bloody Hundredth.' The base was under USAAF control from June 1943 to the end of the war. Some of the airfield survives today, and it is the home of the 100th Bomb Group Memorial Museum. Source: Imperial War Museum, American Air Museum, www.america-nairmuseum.com/place/373.

right into each other and we lost something like 31 planes—you couldn't see where you were going or anything. Worst feeling in the world; that was probably even hairier than the day I was shot down.

Anyway, we were in the lead group, and on the previous mission, we had lost one engine and we had to borrow a different squadron's plane to go on this particular mission on the 6th of March. If you had a crew able to go, and another squadron had a plane that was in mechanical good condition and yours wasn't, you went up in the other plane. It happened to be an 'all-out effort,' so General Doolittle didn't care who he sent up there; he sent us up there, 810 bombers, I think, and it was like 150 fighters or something like that. Out of those 810 bombers, we lost 69. Out of our group alone, we lost 15; most of that was due to German fighters.

Our group had taken off with thirty-six planes, six of which aborted because of mechanical problems. Out of the thirty that continued on, only fifteen got to the target. Out of those fifteen, I guess only a handful ever got back to our base, because they all scattered to different groups.

Our fighter support went a short ways with us, but they weren't there at that time. We were lead group. When you have that many planes in the air and that few fighters, you couldn't get them all. We got shot down around noontime by a Messerschmitt. I was in the top turret shooting at them, and I could see [their faces] as clearly as I'm looking at you. They wiped us out completely.

Our particular squadron, the 349th, was lead squadron that day, but when we borrowed this particular plane from the 351st, they stuck us with that squadron. We filled in on the triangle of the 351st; they put us in the last plane in their squadron because we didn't belong to them. You can visualize the lower element being four planes. [Gestures with hands] One, then two on the side, and one on the bottom. That's where we were, and on the Messerschmitt's first pass, he knocked out those first three planes! Also, he hit the lead plane, knocked it out—hit the tail. The guys survived and got back to England, but the fighter knocked up their dorsal fin. They came in, they didn't care; they were just very [bold] because they didn't want us to get to Berlin.

'They just devastated us'

Now this is noon, March 6, a very clear, bright, sunny day, very cold. Being the last plane in the element, of course, I was panning behind us, and as I'm turning I can see some flashes out of a waist gunner from one of the planes above in the upper element. I whipped the gun around as fast as I could from the back of the plane to the front of the plane, my twin .50s, and I just caught the fighters coming in, right out of the sunlight; they came swooping in wingtip to wingtip. You see, they had learned different tactics. Earlier in the war they would just dive in one after another. Well, one after another you could shoot each one at a time, but coming in this way they just strafed the whole group. They just devastated us.

Anyway, as I'm firing the top turret at them, they're coming over, and we're the last ones, so now he's pulling up. As he's pulling up and making his turn, I'm following him the same way. God as my witness, as I'm following for a split couple of seconds or so, he's banking this way, I'm banking with him. I'm looking at him and he's looking at me. You could see him looking over with his mask on, and he could see me obviously. I'm following him with the damn turret and you could see bits of the plane coming off his tail section, but not enough to bother him. As I'm turning, the electrical cord on my flying suit got caught underneath the swivel of the turret. As it got caught on the swivel of the turret, I couldn't turn it anymore.

The first thing I needed to do was to get down and untangle it. I ducked down, I untangled it, and right beneath the flight deck, the canvas over the gyro-equipment was on fire from a tracer round from the enemy. I took an extinguisher and I put the fire out. This couldn't have taken any more than two or three minutes, whatever it was. I put that out. Now I got back into my turret. Fellas, the turret wasn't there anymore. That son-of-a-gun who had been eyeing me came in and he hit his 20mm gun, took the top of that Plexiglas and tore it right off! Now I get up there, my guns are immobilized, and there's no turret! That's when I say, 'Oh boy.'

I got down; now I'm helpless. Now we're defenseless. The planes ahead of us have been shot down, we're lumbering along at 180 miles an hour, and these fighters were just [warming up] for target practice.

I got up between the pilot and copilot where I generally stand. I said to Lt. Coper, the pilot, 'Hey, Cope, I see some clouds down there about 10,000 feet below us. Dive down for those clouds.'

In the meantime my bombardier comes down, and he's just a step down to the front of the plane. He's a big fella, about 6'1 or 6'2. He says, 'Hey, Charlie, what are we going to do?'

[In the heat of things], I forgot about him, completely forgot about him. His flying clothes were all shredded like a cat had scratched him, from shrapnel, but he wasn't injured. I looked at him. I said, 'What the hell do you want from me? Bail out!' After I saw him in the [German] hospital later, he told me he kicked out the navigator's hatch right then, which was fortunate for him because when it was time for me to jump, I couldn't get out of the plane because the plane was in a spin.

I'm there for another three or four minutes when the fighters make another pass. In the meantime, they hit a couple of our engines; I think number three was on fire. Finally, they made another pass and they shot away our controls! We peeled off into one of these spirals—you've seen them on television where the plane will come over on its back and just spiral into the ground. That's when

I decided it was time to get out; [the whole time before] I figured we'd get back home—you know, optimistic. I didn't figure we were going to [crash].

We were at 21-22,000 feet when this happened. Anyway, I grabbed a hold of a chest pack parachute, because in a turret you can't wear a chest pack, there's not enough room. Trees are coming up at me, and I can't get the damn thing situated! The plane kind of gave a lurch, and all of a sudden I got it snapped on. I had my hand on the ripcord and out I went, headfirst.

Ordinarily the navigator's hatch is a couple of feet behind the number two propeller. Because we were spinning in, you're going down, so now you're actually going into the prop. I did half a flip; my foot was out and the prop caught my foot, split my foot right down the middle!

I pulled the ripcord as soon as I went out, and the chute opened immediately, and I said to myself, 'I don't want to drag my foot.' I landed, and as God is my witness, I landed just like I stepped off this chair, into a plowed field. Never had a chance to look up at the parachute silk or even down at the ground. My copilot went out right after me and he landed about 50 feet away, and about another 100 feet from him was where the plane crashed. That's how close to the ground we were; [none of the others got out of the plane in time]. Now I'm on the ground and this foot is split wide open. I hobble over to my parachute silk, and we're trying to tie a tourniquet around my leg when the bombs start popping. We were carrying twelve 500-pounders. There were some trees in between us, and every time they would go off, the shrapnel would come down like rainfall.

Anyway, we had just missed this farmhouse. We were in this field in northern Germany. The people from the farmhouse, they had little shelter. They had dug a four-foot square hole in the back of their house where they were staying. The only male in the whole contingent was a guy probably running the Home Guard or whatever he was. He came down, and the first thing he asked was if we had a 'pistola' or something. They issued us .45s, but I never carried one. I said, 'Nah, no pistola.'

'That's not Holland, buddy'

You've got to remember this was three months before the invasion, so the whole continent was occupied by the Germans. This was northern Germany. You come over the Channel and you fly through Holland and then you go east into Berlin. Anyway, Gordon, my copilot, the first thing he asked the guy, 'Where are we? Where are we?'

The guy kept saying, 'Deutschland, Deutschland.'

He said, 'Hey, Charlie, we're in luck. This is Holland.' Get this, the queerest thing about this is the copilot was of German descent, but he didn't understand a word of German. I said, 'Nice going, Gordon. That's not Holland, buddy.'

Now I'm bleeding pretty good, and these bombs start to go off, and I said, 'Well, we've got to get the hell out of here.' I start hobbling up towards the farmhouse. I jumped on one foot and I had my arm around my copilot. My foot would go this way and my toes would go that way. It was like a squirt gun, blood was coming out so bad. Anyway, I got up there and I was still trying to tie a tourniquet around my ankle where the bones are protecting your veins; I started up there where you've got more access to your veins. I'm starting to lose quite a bit of blood. As a matter of fact, one time, blood was squirting out so bad it would be like a water pistol from here to you. It just squirted right out of me, and that's how it was. I had to put my finger on the vein to stop the thing from squirting. The plane's on fire and the bombs are going off and I'm saying, 'We're about to get killed by our own damn bombs.' I turn around and try to say something to Gordon. Next thing I know, one of the bombs goes off and he's in that trench with those old ladies, lying down. I says, 'So much for help from him.'

I hobbled over to this farmhouse, which was maybe fifty feet away from this trench. It was an old farmhouse with a big barn attached to the kitchen. I got into the kitchen and they had some ladder back chairs. I took two of the ladder back chairs, turned them around, leaned back, and had my foot elevated, and it was enough to make me come back to my senses a little bit because I was starting to feel real faint. A short time later, two German soldiers came in, and I remember one was real sympathetic and the other was a little hard-nose, which wasn't too bad, because one out of two ain't bad.

One guy was saying, 'We'll take you to see a doctor.'

I said, 'Well, please.'

The other guy was telling me, 'Well, you should have thought about that before you took off,' or something like that.

Anyway, this one guy, here he sees my foot, so he starts sprinkling this sulfanilamide powder on it. At least he got it on there, right? They took me to a little crossroads in this little farm country.

Now you've got to remember, we were one of the lead groups; this was at noon, and we're still flying over. You've got eight hundred and ten B-17s and B-24s. If you were standing there watching the lead group go by for the whole mission, it would take you three hours before the last plane would fly over that particular position. That's how many planes came over; it was an 'all-out effort.' We had little spaces in between but you would have that many planes. Later on, as we got control and they produced more planes, the missions got a little heavier where you had thousand-plane raids. You've got all the German Air Force shooting, and it's like the Fourth of July. From the ground, it's noisier than hell, and then everything they shoot up comes down again, the artillery and flak and everything else. You could see why the people are really desperate down below.

The Operation

They took me to this little infirmary, and they had me on this metal operating table, and some guy with a flak helmet comes in. He severed my toes and tied the foot up. My big toe and the next toe were lying there by themselves in an enamel pan, but even then I was grateful. They did it without any anesthetic, which didn't bother me, because I didn't know what the hell this was about. Those German doctors that operated on me March 6, I never had anything else done to that foot since then, so it had to be pretty good. Today, similar circumstances with the toes still hanging on, they probably would have done microsurgery and probably would have stitched them together, but you've got to remember this goes back 56, 57 years.

They wrapped it up and they put me in an ambulance, sent me to a hospital in Oldenburg there, which was a secondary hospital. We were practically the first prisoners that they ever saw, and this was March 6, '44. They operated on me [again]. Of course, I had anesthetic then; they gave me some ether and stuff. I remember the two surgeons that did the operation, one was a captain and one was a first lieutenant, and they were both graduates from Heidelberg Medical School. I thanked them later on, and then I remember the younger guy sitting next to me while I was lying there. 'Well, we're first doctors,' he says, 'then we're soldiers.' Which meant he was going to take care of us.

He also asked me how many missions I was on. Of course, I said, 'Ah, that was my first one.' It didn't make any difference. They knew more about me than I knew about myself.

About thirty days later I was interrogated down there in Frank-furt. I remember the ride in this railroad car. For the last couple of days we hadn't had anything to eat, and we got into this interroga-tion center. One of the guards there put me in this little room, little cell. I said to him, in German, 'Hey, buddy.' I'd been there long enough to know a couple of words in German. I evidently got through pretty good with those few words, because he hollered over, 'Hey, we've got a German from Brooklyn here.' [*Laughs*]

I said, in German, 'I'm just hungry.'

He said, 'Okay, I'll take care of you.' He made me believe that.

I went in and got interrogated; this first lieutenant interrogated me. He spoke English quite well. He could have been reading the list of my whole crew.

I said, 'Hey, wait a minute. Tell me, did these guys pass through here?'

He wouldn't answer me, but they didn't. I was asking him ques-tions whether or not some of those boys were there. Of course, they weren't. They were all killed; just the three of us got out. There was no way for them to get out. I was fortunate to get out because I was in front of the hatch and we were up front, but in the back it was whipping pretty bad. In other words, he knew my whole crew and all their names and previous records before I even took off. They asked me different things, and I asked him more questions than he asked me.

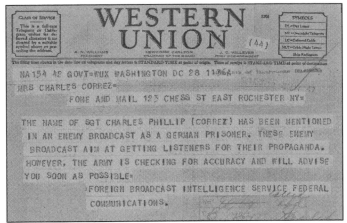

Misspelled notice to Corea family giving update
on Charlie's PoW status. Photo: Corea family.

Stalag 17

They sent us to Stalag 17-B, the world famous Stalag 17. They made a movie about it.[44] It was down in Krems, Austria, 40 kilometers west of Vienna. They had some of the first PoWs of the war—there were some there who were captured in North Africa. [But] most of us in our compound were all Air Force, non-commissioned officers, mostly 8th Air Force but 15th Air Force too. They also had French, Italians, and Russians, but they had different compounds.

We had an upper and lower level, with the center being the washrooms. Of course, they had double bunks. I was up in the infirmary for about 10 months, which was a break in that respect. The regular compound had these barracks—big washroom, lower barracks. Then they had a big, open field and they had a big latrine that took care of different barracks in the center. Then, of course, they had the main compound where you could walk around. Of course,

---

[44] *Stalag 17-* 1953 Oscar-winning film which tells the story of a group of American airmen in this PoW camp.

you were way out in no man's land; there was nothing but farmland around you.

Charlie Corea, photo in captivity.
Photo: Corea family.

The conditions inside the barracks were kind of barren. I didn't get down there until about 10 months after I was a prisoner. They had some crystal sets that they were getting some information through BBC at night. What they would do is, after they turn the lights out, they would connect the antennas to the electrical circuit and use the electrical circuit as a big antenna. Then they would have this happen in maybe just one barrack or so. Then whatever news, they would come around and somebody would read it to us, that the war's going this way or that way. That was it, and, of course, we weren't allowed to work and we ended up with these parcels that the Red Cross gave us. We were fortunate, being down in Austria, close to Switzerland; that's where they were being distributed, through Switzerland. For the most part we were getting one package a week, and that took care of us pretty good. Later on, as things got a little hairy, you got maybe one package for two people. I don't know if you're familiar with it. It had a can of Spam, a ration of biscuits that looked like graham crackers, only very highly concentrated, and a good-size package of that. They had a two-ounce can of instant coffee, a larger can of dry milk, called 'Klim,' which is milk spelled backwards. It had a quarter-pound bar of cheese—sometimes you'd get Velveeta, sometimes you'd get American—along with a two-ounce can of jam or jelly, grape or strawberry or whatever. Five packs of cigarettes, and two D bars. D bars were like these great big Hershey bars, only they were thick and heavily concentrated—we used to have contests of how many you could eat before you threw up or something like that. [*Laughs*] Anyway, we used those D bars, they were our medium of exchange. The D bar was our gold standard and it was pretty good, like a can of strawberry jam, which was probably the most popular jam. If somebody wanted something, he may say, 'Look, I'll give you a D bar or a pack of cigarettes for it,' or something like that. The cigarettes were great, especially for bartering. I was a smoker, but not that much of a smoker. These Russians were in the compound next to us, and, of course, there was about three rows of wire between us. We could yell over, and they had a warning wire and everything else. They were workers. They would send them out to the farms and they would work in the fields, and, of course, they would bring home a package of onions, carrots, molasses, and stuff like that. I don't know where they got the molasses, but we would trade, and, of course, they didn't have no smokes at all. We'd fling over a pack of cigarettes, and they'd fling over a bag of onions or package of onions or carrots or potatoes; whatever they had, you know.

The Germans didn't mind too much, but the unfortunate thing was, you know, later in the war, some of the guards were a little younger and immature. I remember one of the times somebody threw over a pack of cigarettes towards the Russian barracks. This guy was in the window and he didn't quite get it, and it fell down below outside the barrack, which was inside the warning wire compound. Of course, the Russians had a more ruthless life anyway. The guy thought nothing of jumping down and picking it up and jumping back in.

Well, this particular day, this one young guard was over there, and he fired from the hip and happened to hit the guy as he was crawling back into the window. Killed him and let him lie there for half a day or so. The Germans transferred the guard the next day.

What we would [normally] do if something happened where a Russian would throw a bag of onions, say, and we had 20 feet of warning wire [and it fell short], we would bribe the guard to kick it over. You know what I mean? He'd say, 'What the heck.' It didn't bother him, so you'd give the guard a couple of cigarettes or something like that.

I never received any mail. For some reason it never got to me, but some of my mail got to my folks; I still have them. You didn't write too much, and I wouldn't worry my mother, just 'everything's fine and I'm okay.' They would block out anything else anyway. That part of it. I know my family was telling me that they would, back in those days, they'd go up to a place like Sibley's Department Store, and they used to have these packages for PoWs, and they would send whatever they got there; [I didn't see it]. But there were people who got their mail.

The End of the War

[Near the end of the war], the Germans were fighting a defending action against the Russians, along the Danube Road there. We were just north of the Danube. They decided to move the American prisoners out of camp towards Linz, Austria. Linz was the dividing line that passed down the agreement between Russia and the

United States that General Patton couldn't go any farther than that. He was at Linz, Austria, which was 60 kilometers northwest of us.

These last remaining Germans who were in charge of camp, they didn't want to be taken over by the Russians, naturally. They moved [everyone] out of the camp except for us wounded non-ambulatory people that were left, about 80 of us. They moved them out and marched them out of camp. We, of course, said goodbye. We figured, 'We'll see you. We're going back with Uncle Joe,' you know, Joe Stalin; we were naïve enough to think that he was a great guy. [Laughs] 'We'll see you when we get back,' and all that. When they moved a camp out and all the German officers left, a couple of guys went up to the headquarters and got some records. They got my service record and they got a little radio that was up there, and we got listening to the news.

We were all bunched up in this one part of the infirmary up on the hill. Of course, [the Germans] had supplies that Red Cross had sent and the mail up there that had never been distributed. There were packages that were sent to the prisoners [who were now evacuated], and I remember ending up with a couple boxes of Philly cigars and a brand-new baseball uniform that the Salvation Army had sent! Here they are, these beautiful white flannel baseball uniforms, pure white; I ended up wearing one of these white flannel uniforms, and I had a cigar. Then in marched some Russian or Jewish slave labor, I don't know what, to take the barracks that had been evacuated. We're on this side of the fence and we're watching these people come in. I'm a hell of a sight—here I am smoking a Philly cigar in a white baseball uniform, throwing cigarettes at these poor bastards who were coming across. You're twenty-two years old, what the heck. [Chuckles]

Anyway, these Russian troops came over into camp, and we were on the hillside, and they camped just on the high side. Our smiles went away pretty fast, because now [the Germans] are shelling the Russians from the top of the hill, and the Russians are going to shell them, and we're right in the middle! You've got about 80 Air Force guys trying to dig a foxhole! [*Laughs*] That was kind of scary, because the night that our GIs moved out, what they couldn't carry they decided to burn out in front of the barracks— planks, I don't know why. They just decided to burn what they couldn't take with them. So, of course, that night the ashes were smoldering. The Germans were still fighting this retreating action, so some night fighters see this, strafed the hell out of us. They could see these flickering lights, and the Russians are only a mile or two down in the same area. It got a little hairy, and that's when they even killed a couple of Germans, our guards.

The next day, we were in the top part of the barracks. Dangling out of the ceiling were all these cluster bombs that didn't go off. They looked like Christmas ornaments; that's how close it was! It got a little hairy right about then, because here we are, the war's over. We listened on BBC that night, I think May 7. *'At twelve o'clock the war will be officially over.'* No sooner had [the announcer] gotten that out of his mouth, this night fighter comes over and drops these cluster bombs like crazy [again]!

*

[The war's over.] For three or four days, we're in limbo here. The guys who went out to [try to arrange] our transportation, they didn't show up. What happened was they got to Linz and reported in, [told them] to pick up some American prisoners, so a convoy of three or four trucks was sent out to pick us up. They never notified the Russians. The treaty was 'don't go beyond that [line on the map].' The Russians knocked out the convoy! Then [our guys] had to go back and regroup the convoy—it was a week later we finally got taken out of there, and it's only 60 kilometers.

I got to go into the little town [near the camp] and visit some of the local people there; the Russians had come over by then. They were in the field and we walked right by them; they hardly looked up at us. Some of those cannons they had were horse-drawn. Couldn't believe it! They were sitting there eating whatever they had in their hand.

We were looking for maybe a bottle of wine; we asked the local people. I remember one family asking us to stay overnight. It's kind of funny. We found out the reason was they had a couple of young women there, their daughters. They figured if the Americans stayed overnight those scrubby Russians wouldn't come in and do who-knows-what to them. I don't remember if we stayed the night; I don't think I did.

Finally, we got out of there and got to Linz, Austria. We were flown out of Linz, Austria, to Camp Lucky Strike. We were supposed to fly home, but we finally went home by boat. We went home by an old cruise ship, the *Manhattan* or *American* or something like that. Anyway, there were a lot of experiences in between, naturally, but I could stay here for a week and talk to you about it.

*

'That's how I feel about it'

It's a funny thing when you get me talking about stuff like this. I can remember experiences, but if you ask me something that happened two days ago, like my wife will ask something, and I say, 'I don't remember.' That's what happens when you're eighty years old. You have old memories....

Charlie Corea.
Photo: Corea family.

I think I was very fortunate. Like everything in the military, you can get a medal for this, and a medal for that—it's just a matter of being in the right place at the right time, or in the wrong place. Like I just said, I received some awards, and the last one I got was for a state award. A young girl reporter asked me something about the war, about why did you get this.

She says, 'Well, you know you're quite a hero.'

I said, 'I'm not a hero. I have seven guys on my crew that were killed. How can I be a hero? I was lucky to get out. I was just a victim of circumstances.'

We got on talking about how I was lucky when I got out. The Germans operated on me and saved my foot and all that.

She said, 'Why would they do that?'

'Well, what do you mean?'

'Why would they take care of you?' That's how naïve these youngsters are.

I said, 'Well, there's a Geneva Convention that they had, and we take care of their prisoners and they hopefully take care of ours.' She couldn't understand.

'You're over there bombing them, and now you want them to take care of you.'

I said, 'Well, that's just the way it is. Stupid war. It's just the way it is. You get medals stupidly. You happen to be in the right place, you get a medal.'

That's how I feel about it. This is one of the very few times where I even talk about this... I get 30% disability. I'm sure if you saw my foot, I could probably get more. The system is there to be plucked if you want to pluck it, but I worked hard making a living while I was raising four children. You know what I mean?

[I look around today and] to me, sometimes I think it isn't worth it. [But then again], and I was telling this to a friend of mine the other day, when all my friends and buddies and classmates entered the service back in 1942, right after Pearl Harbor, there was no doubt about what we had to do. I've never seen that much cooperation and patriotism until September 11th. That's the only good thing that came out of September 11th, the country coming together like it did back in 1941. That's the closest feeling that I had to that, since.

[My friends and I], we went into the service, got out, we went on to college [or work]... I ran a little business, I published a paper, 39 years. I raised a family, put them through school, boom, boom— and all of a sudden we're eighty years old. I don't feel 80, but I'm 80. You'll find out as you get older, how fast time goes. You already realize that, right?

"I read The Greatest Generation. *I read three or four chapters of that. I put the book down. Somebody said, 'Why didn't you finish? Didn't you like it?'*

I said, 'No, I didn't finish, because everything he said was true and I already knew about it.' We all did the same thing; we all did what we had to do."

Charlie Corea passed away at the age of 92 on August 26, 2014.

Earl Morrow, Sam Lisica, Jerry Silverman. July 2001.
Credit: Author.

CHAPTER SEVEN

B-17 PoW Reunion

Earl M. Morrow was born in 1921 and was featured in Book One of The War in the Air, *detailing his early missions and all about the day that the B-17 bomber he was commanding was shot down, and his experiences that followed. In the summer of 2001, two of his World War II buddies came to his house to celebrate his 80th birthday. Earl asked me if I wanted to meet them, and I grabbed my video camera and headed over to sit with the three of them around Earl's dining room table. I interviewed him and the others, Sam Lisica of Pennsylvania and Jerome Silverman of Long Island, all formerly of the 457th Bomb Group of the U.S. Eighth Army Air Force during World War II.*

All of them had been taken prisoner on November 2, 1944, near Volkstedt, in Germany, when their planes were shot down. Earl was the pilot and Sam was the bombardier on the B-17 'Delores' #4337766; Jerry was aboard the lead plane as the lead navigator for the mission that day and was picked up on the ground by enemy forces, winding up in the same German transport vehicle as Earl, where they met for the first time. This meeting was the first time in seven years that Earl and Sam had seen each other; Sam, who had bunked with Jerry in the PoW camp, had not seen Jerry since the end of the war. We sat at the dining room table at Earl Morrow's home. I set up my video camera; Earl, the pilot, was in another room, searching for some photographs. I began the conversation by asking some questions. It would turn out to be their last time together.

*

Together Again

Earl Morrow, pilot, 80
Sam Lisica, bombardier, 80
Jerry Silverman, navigator, 82

Matthew Rozell, interviewer: You were in the U.S. Army Air Force?

Sam Lisica, bombardier: The United States Army Air Corps, [in the beginning].

[Earl Morrow enters the room with a crew photograph]

Earl Morrow, pilot: We got lucky; I found it.

Sam, bombardier: That's the one we got in 1944.

Interviewer: You each got one?

Earl, pilot: Yes.

Jerry Silverman, navigator: Well, I don't have it with me. I showed a picture like that [to a young girl], and I said, 'You know when you see the parades and you see all these old people, these people marching with the flags and the hats and all? When you pass the cemetery and you see all the old people, grandmas and grandpas in the cemetery? Well, all those graves, the kids were 18, 19 and 20 years old...' Then I [showed the photograph], and I said, 'Next time you see a parade of old geezers, this guy here was 18, flying combat, this guy was 19, flying combat...'

Earl, pilot: [points to picture] This man here was 18.

Sam, bombardier: Yes, he just came out of high school. He was the waist gunner; he died the day we went down.

Earl, pilot: These three were killed the day we went down. This one retired in the 1980s as a brigadier general.

Interviewer: Which one are you?

Earl, pilot: [*pointing*] This is me, this is Sam, Bob; George is gone, Bill is gone, he was shot up real bad, but we got him out and he survived and he died in about 1978 or 1979—he was playing golf and he had a heart attack. George, the one next to him, he just passed away two years ago.

*Crew photograph. Front row far left-Earl Morrow. Far right-Sam Lisica.
Courtesy Earl Morrow.*

Jerry, navigator, to interviewer: See that picture? Every crew had a picture like that; the army did that. The four in the front were generally the pilot, the copilot, the bombardier, and the navigator, or vice versa. These would be the enlisted men here [*pointing to top row in crew photo*]. See, these are the enlisted men, [and in the front], these are the officers.

Earl, pilot: [*pointing*] Radioman, waist gunner, top turret gunner, waist gunner, ball turret gunner; these two switched off and on and they were both killed. This other guy was qualified as an engineer also, but he didn't go with us that day. This is the tail gunner...

Sam, bombardier: We had ten men, but only nine flew, so every mission, someone would [sit it out]. Did you just have ten men in your crew?

Jerry, navigator: Oh yes.

Earl, pilot: In our group, they always pulled one waist gunner and left him home. One crew member stayed home.

Jerry, navigator: Never with us; we always had ten. I never flew a mission with nine people. Back when I was leading, we had two or three navigators [aboard one plane].

Earl, pilot: Well, they probably needed them, with you. [*Laughter*]

Jerry, navigator: If you're leading a group, it's one thing, but if you're leading a division or a wing, that's another one.[45] One was the lead navigator, one was the DR navigator, and one would just read our radar. [46]

Earl, pilot: You see, when we got over there, we always left one guy home, because we pulled the gunner off the radio, so if you get under attack, he goes back to the waist...

Jerry, navigator: You always have two waist guns, always.

Sam, bombardier: We had one.

---

[45] *leading a group, it's one thing, but if you're leading a division or a wing, that's another one*-Silverman refers to the size of the strike force a lead crew would be responsible for. A B-17 'squadron' might be six planes; by 1943, a heavy bomb 'group' included nearly 300 officers and 1,500 enlisted men to fly and service 48 B-17 bombers. Their 'wing' included 3 such groups.
[46] *DR navigator*-dead reckoning is the process of calculating one's position by estimating direction and distance traveled by using a previously determined 'fix' (position) and advancing that position based upon estimated speeds over time and course, rather than by electronic navigation methods.

Earl, pilot: [*pointing*] See, that's why Bellinger wasn't with us the day we were shot down.

Jerry, navigator: I was amazed at how many rounds I could shoot off. We went onto the back of the ship; you could kill yourself on all the shells all over the place—they're like marbles all over the place! You have to remember at this point I was the lead navigator and I didn't have any clue who I flew with; I didn't know any of these guys.

Earl, pilot: Yes, well, you flew in lead crews; it didn't pertain to you, what happened to us.

Jerry, navigator: My original crew had long since went home; the co-pilot and I came back for a second tour, but he and I didn't fly together because he was on a new lead crew, and he was on a crew that flew together.

Interviewer, referring to Jerry: You were the navigator, right?

Sam, bombardier: Group navigator.

Jerry, navigator: No, I was not a group navigator.

Earl, pilot: Squadron navigator.

Jerry, navigator: And I wasn't a squadron navigator.

Sam, bombardier: Lead navigator?

Jerry, navigator: No, not at that time.

Earl, pilot: What was your title then?

Jerry, navigator: I was a specialist navigator, but I navigated as a lead navigator. He's got more experience. They put you more forward—to lead the pack—because we always went in groups. There was the lead navigator, and the lead bombardier. We had to fly the target and help the bombardier fly close to the target.

Earl, pilot, to interviewer: And all we really needed to do was to follow the lead ship.

Jerry, navigator: We had to look at the [reconnaissance] pictures and see what the Germans were doing. A river would be like this [*mimics bends in a 'river' by snaking his hand across the tabletop*], and the target would be here [*gestures to a point on his 'river'*]. Many times we would have problems with clouds under us because we flew 20,000 to 25,000 feet. There would be a hole in the clouds, and [the Germans] would set up a whole city, a dummy [*decoy*].

[*Interviewer looks at him with incredulous expression*]

Really! If you see a hole in the clouds and you see this, you think this is it, that this is the target. It's a bend in the river the same as this; they'd duplicate it! There was a movie, *Command Decision* with Walter Pigeon, and it's exactly what happened to the navigator! They thought they hit the target and they got all excited, and then the navigator says that it's 'gross error.' He says, 'That was a dummy I hit.' It's in the movie.

And I'll tell you one thing, and this is documented. The Eighth Air Force—I don't know about the others, but I imagine the same thing—we would never turn back from a raid.

Interviewer: Why not?

Sam, bombardier: If we were told to go, we just went.

Jerry, navigator: The only time we turned back was because of really bad weather. That was the only thing. We had a recall for weather.

Earl, pilot: We couldn't see the ground unless we had the new radar, which they were just coming in with. There was no way to hit the target.

Jerry, navigator: Well, we still bombed; we just bombed through the clouds. On those days there was never really bad opposition from flak or fighters. We in the Air Command would say, 'We can't back up.' In the Air Command, it's not like the infantry; you can't say, 'Let's back up and regroup.'

8th AF B-17 Flying Fortresses, 396th Bomb Group, 1943.
Credit: USAF. Library of Congress, public domain.

Missions

Jerry, navigator: When we were in the air, we never turned back. They would put up so much flak, and we would never go around it before we hit another target. We went through the flak, straight for that target—we never dodged it. Each time we went through, we lost 50, 60, 70 bombers at a time, each carrying 10 men, and at the end of 1943 and three raids, if we had two more raids like that, we would have had no more Air Force. We would have been completely wiped out. So they just stood down.

Sam, bombardier: The RAF thought we were crazy; we thought they were crazy. Always doing it at night...

Jerry, navigator: They had a whole different conception; they bombed at night, but they weren't as heavily armed as we were.

They carried heavier bomb loads—we would never fly at night, it is dangerous as hell! They would never fly in the daytime; they would say you'd get killed doing that.

I copied [our high casualty rate] out of the book about the Eighth Air Force. The author said the Air Force had the highest casualties of any branch of service! I was stunned to read this in another book too, that the Eighth Air Force had more casualties than all of the Marine landings in the Pacific! And that really shook me up—the author states, 'You guys are heroes,' and we're not heroes, but when I read this, I decided, 'I am a damn hero.'

Interviewer: You must have lost a lot of friends. How did you deal with that?

Jerry, navigator: The way it was dealt with in many cases with the officers and the enlisted men—they were together, and then these guys finished up [*gestures to Sam and Earl*], and my guys finished up. And I went home after so many missions, 'rest and recuperation,' 'R&R,' which we called 'return and regret'—but anyway, we got through the thing. What happened when a crew went down, and replacements came through, was that word started getting around— 'Don't get friendly with these guys because it breaks your heart,' you know, so no one talked to anybody. But anyway, we got through the thing.

*

Interviewer: When you went over to England, who flew with Earl before you all got shot down?

Sam, bombardier: [*points to Earl, pilot*] We were the crew men on that plane.

Interviewer: Clarification—you two guys were on the same crew, that's why I have you in this photograph, and you had 17 missions before you got shot down.

Sam, bombardier: He had 17; I had 23.

Earl, pilot: There was a little period there where I got grounded.

Sam, bombardier: They were going to shoot him. [*Laughter*]

Earl, pilot: I tore up two airplanes one morning—wrecked them while we were taking off. It's simple, I just caught the tail section of the airplane in front of me with the wing tip, because we came up this taxiway and there was a portable tower sitting there, and we got into our right turn behind the next airplane, and we had no brakes—everything was gone! The tail wheel was turned, to keep us turned to the right. Well, we don't want to really tear up that tower there, and the airplane's in front of me and the tail's wrong, so at the last second, just to save everything we could, I had to gun the hell out of the two right engines and swing her around, and my wing tip caught the tail of one of the planes in front of me.

Sam, bombardier: Took the rudder off.

Earl, pilot: The problem was, the night before, someone came in and landed and took a building off its foundation! And the colonel said, 'Next time there is an incident, it'll be pilot error, one hundred percent,' and it was me. I fall into those things...

Jerry, navigator: The commanding officer of any unit is responsible, no matter what, and the pilot is responsible. Now if the mechanic does something wrong and the pilot, he's sleeping, and the mechanic is working at two o'clock in the morning, working on that airplane to get it ready, if something goes wrong, the end result in all commanding officers' opinions is that he's the pilot [*points to Earl*], he's responsible. In other words, Harry Truman later said, 'The buck stops here,' and that's what happened. Unfortunately, he had something mechanically wrong, but even though he didn't know anything, [in the colonel's eyes], it's going to be pilot error; otherwise some general's going to say, 'Colonel, what's going on?' He would then 'pass the buck.'

Earl, pilot: The co-pilot makes a mistake, and it's my fault for letting him make it. So you know when you get up there, you take the guff. So that's why we didn't come up with the same number of missions.

Jerry, navigator: [agreeing] That's why you didn't have the same number of missions.

Earl, pilot: Another reason is when I first got there, when I went on my first mission, I went out as a co-pilot with an experienced crew. The next day I went out as pilot, and I got all my crew, except my co-pilot; I got an experienced co-pilot. On the third mission, the crew was on its own.

Jerry, navigator: I came over before he did. When a group came over originally, you came over in one group. As you lost people, you got replacements. They [*Earl and Sam*] came over as another crew, as a replacement crew.

Interviewer: Were you at the same base?

Jerry, navigator: Same base, same squadron, same everything. So a whole crew got shot down, they put another crew in their beds.

Interviewer: Did you know them at all before?

Jerry, navigator: No, I never knew them. I had been there a while; I had never set eyes on them. Anyway, I came home; I've completed one tour, came home on what they call 'rest and recuperation.'

After 25 missions I could go home on leave. I could fly five more and stay home for good, or I could fly 25, go on leave, and come back again. If I chose to fly to thirty, I figured I could get killed on number 26, 27, 28, et cetera. I figured 'take what you got', you know, 'take your winnings and get off the table.' So I went home, and then I came back. Now I didn't come back [to my original] crew. I came back as a lead navigator, and I was put on as a lead crew navigator. They have crews who were trained to lead, they have other guys that come in to navigate. On the lead plane they had two guys navigating, one guy looking out the window, another guy doing the paperwork, the third guy was on the radio to make it as good as we possibly could get it.

I came back onto my second tour, and each time I flew, I flew with different people. I didn't even know the people I was on the plane with that day, but that's just the way it works. You know, when you fly, you have specialists: you have a special bombardier; the best bombardier in a crew, that sort of thing. What happened was here we are in a group of 36 aircraft in our combat box. We had twelve and twelve and twelve, so we were in the same unit. It was called a 'low box'; they called it a box because twelve [points up], twelve [points middle], and twelve [points low]—high box, lead box, and low box. When the Germans came, they came from behind, and they hit the low box and they took out seven planes, plus two more from our squadron.

*

Shot Down

Interviewer: And what was the target when you were shot down? It was November of '44, right?

Earl, pilot: It was November 2, 1944.

Jerry, navigator: Merseburg.

Earl, pilot: Merseburg synthetic oil field.

Interviewer: You were brought down by fighter planes?

Jerry, navigator: Fighters, yes. We got hit from behind—I never saw them. I heard the crew yelling, then the shooting, everything going on back there—I'm up at the front of the plane, this is going on in the tail. The Germans, at this point—previously they used to come in and attack individually—but at this point in the war they didn't have the gas to train their pilots, number one; number two, they didn't have a safe place to train them because our fighters were ranging all over, so they had inexperienced pilots. So they would take a few good pilots and tell the rest of the guys to 'String out and stick with us,' so they just hit us in waves. And the first thing I knew,

I see little 'cotton balls' in the air, which are 40mm cannons exploding, which I haven't seen before, and then an airplane hit ours, or one of their fighters hit our wing. I didn't see it happen, but I felt the whole airplane shake, and I said, 'What happened?', and something hit our wing—the plane was on fire, and we bailed out.

Sam, bombardier: I was hurt. When I hit the ground, I bruised my left knee. It was huge and it was all swollen, and I walked with a limp. I don't know if you were with me [*points to Earl*].

Earl, pilot: No, it wasn't me.

Sam, bombardier: Who the hell was it? I walked across the field, and they made me pick up my chute and carry it, and they took me to the burgermeister's house.

Earl, pilot: The first one I saw on the ground was our tail gunner, and he was the happiest guy on earth to see me. He was afraid that he had bailed out, and the rest of us had gone back to England. When he saw me, he knew he had done the right thing.

Interviewer: He didn't know that the plane blew up?

Earl, pilot: Well, no. But he knew to get out, because he saw the other crew up forward and he motioned for them to go. One guy was left standing there, and he just shook his head. He wasn't going.

Sam, bombardier: And he died. That was one of the guys that died on the plane.

Earl, pilot: And I still think that was strictly a case where—[*reaches for photograph*] Do you see these two small guys here? This guy was in the ball turret. This other one was standing here on the waist gun, and these guys would switch off in the turret. I think they had a deal between them—'If I'm in the turret, you don't leave until I'm out!' And Joe would always stand there and wait for him to get out. And the escape door was gone, and I think Lindquist must have gotten out, and I think he probably was wounded, because when we were on the ground, the Germans came back and told us 'Komrade bleeding,' but they wouldn't let us go to him.[47]

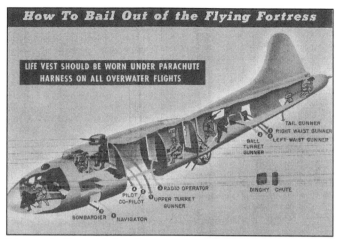

'How to bail out of the Flying Fortress.' B-17 training manual,
U.S. Government. Source: www.cnks.info/b17-flying-fortress-interior

Jerry, navigator: I remember that one. When our plane was hit, it goes with what he's talking about [*points to Earl*]. Our pilot pushed the 'bail out' alarm button and a bell or something rang, and it meant you were supposed to bail out. So I started to bail out and my feet were already hanging out, and I realized that the plane was still flying straight and level. Everybody knew that many a time half the crew bailed out, and the rest of them somehow got back to England! So I figured, this thing is still straight and level. So I came back into the plane and hooked up to the interphone, I got an oxygen bottle, and I called the pilot and said, 'What's wrong with the airplane? We're still going straight and level.'

He said, 'We're on fire.'

---

[47] *the Germans came back and told us 'Komrade bleeding,' but they wouldn't let us go to him*-Radio operator Charles Lindquist, 20, of Iowa, Joseph Salerno, 16, of Michigan, and Robert Koerner, 22, of Kansas, are listed as KIA November 2, 1944.

I said, 'Where?'

He said, 'The waist.'

I crawled through the bomb bay and back, and I haven't crawled through a bomb bay since then, and I don't know how the hell I ever did it the first time, because you can't get through that bomb bay today; maybe I'm a little bigger now, I don't know. But anyway, I opened the door in the back and I see flames—from the radio room on back, it was just solid flame! I closed the door, came forward, curved straight over, and I bailed out. They tell me that the airplane blew up about a little after the last parachute was seen. The part that I forgot was that we were in this big room, and this was three or four hours after we landed, and then I got the shakes [*shakes his hands vigorously*], you know, my nerves were such—up until then I was perfectly normal, as normal as I am sitting here now, and about four hours later it was uncontrollable! I guess it must have been a delayed reaction.

Interviewer: Did all of your crew make it out of the plane?

Jerry, navigator: Everybody got out of our airplane. But the tail gunner that day… He was a lieutenant in the lead plane; the copilot flies in the back position and he polices the formation, he calls off whatever he sees, telling other planes [over the radio] to tighten up their formation. He was the eyes in the back of the pilot's head. He became a 'streamer,' which means he bailed out and popped his parachute, and the parachute came up, but it didn't blossom. It just streamed, so he went down. His name was Ford. I don't know his first name, but his name was Ford.

B-17 Flying Fortresses 486th Bomb Group near Merseburg, November 1944. Credit: USAAF, public domain.

Earl, pilot, to interviewer: [*pointing at photo in National Geographic Magazine*] You saw this picture, didn't you?

Sam, bombardier: That was the same day we got shot down. November 2, 1944.

Earl, pilot: That's it. That's the day we were shot down. My wife was looking at it and said, 'That's you.' That's what we were going through.

Interviewer: You guys had already dropped your bombs, right?

Earl, pilot: Yes. We had already dropped ours and were five minutes out when we were hit and went down.

Sam, bombardier: That's what happens when you become a bomber. [*Looks up toward heaven with hands clasped*] If you get out, you say, 'Thank you, Lord, for letting me go.'

*

On the Ground

Jerry, navigator: When I got on the ground, he [*points to Earl*] was having his own problems in his plane and they bailed out. When I was on the ground, I got picked up by some civilians. Well, not civilians; they were coming towards me, but there was one guy who was police and they say get in the hands of the police or the military, don't let the civilians get a hold of you, because they have pitchforks and they were pitching things other than hay. I didn't see them, luckily, but there were American fliers hanging by the necks from telephone poles and trees because of what we were.

When we got picked up, they put us on a train and took us to [where] there was a railroad station. That's where we got on a train to go back west of Frankfurt, which was the interrogation center. So they had a number of us, I'd say maybe 15, 20, 30, something like that, and we were guarded by the Luftwaffe. We came into this railroad station and all these Germans were there, and the next thing you know, there was a mob of people screaming and shouting, and the Luftwaffe had their guns and they protected us. That's when we first found out...

Earl, pilot: They finally had to lock us in the building in a room in the basement to keep us away from the civilians.

Jerry, navigator: Had it not been for that, we would have been lynched right there. We would have been lynched right there! Now these are the same people that, come April [1945], when they could smell borsht on the Russians' breaths on one side, and onion on the Americans' breaths on the other, you know, then all of a sudden [*imitates German civilian, shrugging shoulders, palms up*], 'What could we do?' You know, [as if to say], 'What would you do if you were in the same position? You'd do the same thing...'

Earl, pilot: They said, 'If you get shot down, you get under military control as soon as you possibly can.'

When we were shot down, the only reason I had a .45 strapped to me was that they made sure you had it when you left. And they put some rifles in the back of the airplane in case you crash-landed so you could protect yourself with it. And at the end of all the discussion, when they were telling us how to use this stuff, they said, 'Save a bullet for yourself.' And I would never do that, but I mean, that's the way it was. The civilians were really going after the Air Force.

Sam, bombardier: They did all the killing of the American airmen when they were captured. Not the soldiers, the civilians did that. Strung them up on telephone poles...

Jerry, navigator: It seems to be worldwide. Nobody seems to like the American airmen. The worst thing about being airmen is being caught by the Viet Cong, caught by the Koreans; they'd torture the airmen.

Earl, pilot: I went to an Air Force gathering recently, that's where I met Clarence Dart [*local Tuskegee Airman*]. But beforehand I saw in the paper that there was going to be a German Luftwaffe pilot who was going to be a speaker, and I didn't want to go. So I called and talked to the director of the program, and his wife said, 'Well, forget your problems and come on out and have a good time.' So I went and I stood there when [the former Luftwaffe pilot] made the speech. Now his speech kind of turned me off, because he spent a lot of time explaining that he was not a combat pilot, and at the end of the war he was flying scientists out of the eastern zone back to the western zone so [the Americans] could get them, and so on and so forth. And he was backing himself up that he was a 'good guy.' So then I flat-out asked him, 'Well, tell me this, when our planes were shot down and our guys were in parachutes, why was the German Luftwaffe shooting at our guys with the parachutes?'

'It couldn't have happened,' he said.

'Well, it did happen,' I said. 'I was there and saw it!' And that kind of turned me off... and since I got on him pretty heavy about those German fighters shooting our guys in the parachutes, he kind of avoids me now.

Jerry, navigator: Well, I can prove to you that what he [*points to Earl*] is saying is correct because when I bailed out, I could see two or three other parachutes and about three or four of us were in a group. I heard the chatter of machine guns, and I got terrified and said, 'Oh my God, they're shooting us, they're going to come around and shoot us in our parachutes.' Now, if the story wasn't around, I wouldn't have thought of that, but it just so happened that all this [machine gun] chatter I heard was not them shooting parachutes; it was what they called a 'Lufbery circle,' which was developed in the first World War after a pilot by the name of Lufbery. [*Motions with hands*] Here's an Me-109, he's on the tail of a P-51, who was on the tail of a 109, who was on the tail of a P-51, and if you break out, you've got to try and turn inside [*motions again with hands*] so they can't get at you. All the while they're trying to get inside and shoot you. So the circle gets tighter and tighter and they're all firing at each other, so I couldn't wait to get down from that cloud level and disappear into the clouds below. But up above I could hear the shooting. And when I came through and I saw the planes, the first thing I thought was that they were shooting at the parachutes. And if I didn't think that, then where did I get the thought? From the stories that go around that they did do these things.

Earl, pilot: Well, they found a guy who was shot through the leg down there and he was still in his parachute. I didn't see any American fighters down there, either. Things were rather hectic.

Jerry, navigator: One thing came back to me yesterday that I hadn't thought about for a long time. By the time I got on the ground and we were picked up and put in a building, which Sam remembers and reminded me about—he's the first guy I've seen in years that was in that same building; I've met a lot of PoWs and I never found a guy that was in that building—and he remembers that I was one of the two guys who weren't wounded. Everyone was wounded, one way or another, and some guys were all burned and blackened like chicken.

Interviewer: It must have been terrible.

Jerry, navigator: Well, it wasn't good. Now this is what I'm talking about; I went off on a tangent and I forgot the damn point.

Earl, pilot: Were you going to talk about the first aid kits? They snatched them so quick, we had nothing to take care of our wounded with.

Sam, bombardier: [*referring to the kit*] The German soldiers would come with a knife and cut the whole thing off. It had iodine and bandages, and they took it for their troops. We had nothing for ours.

Interviewer: You said you were one of the two guys who weren't wounded?

Jerry, navigator: Yes.

Sam, bombardier: He and I were trying to figure out how we were going to take care of the rest. We would look for the packs, and there weren't any there. So I would take off my shirt and my undershirt, because I always wear an undershirt, and we cut that up and used it for bandages. Finally we got the Germans to bring us some stuff for wounds. Like the paper you dry your hands with—that's what they were using for bandages! They brought us some grease, and we put as much on our guys as we could. One guy landed on a roof and it collapsed, so he fell 35 feet to the ground and hurt his back and couldn't move. Every time we tried to move him, he was in pain.

Earl, pilot: He was the one I carried across Frankfurt, on my back, and I don't know if he got used to the pain or what, because he never uttered a cry or anything.

*

Prisoners of War

Interviewer: So it was the same exact day, the same mission you were on?

Jerry, navigator: Yes—then we were collected and put with other guys, and then put on a train, and each section was a whole story in itself, what happened here, what happened there. When I got picked up, two German soldiers came around in a Volkswagen, which was like a Jeep, and he [*points to Earl*] is sitting in the back of the thing, and that's where I met him.

Interviewer: What happened when you were on the Jeep?

Jerry, navigator: Well on the Jeep, this one German, the guy riding shotgun, had a patch on his eye. He was a big guy, and he took his watch [*points to Earl*], he took my high school ring, he said he would keep it so some other guy wouldn't just come and steal it from me, and I would get it back after the war.

I'm not going to argue with the guy. He goes over to him [*points to Earl*] to get his pilot wings, and this big dumb jerk [*referring to Earl*], he's pushing the German away, and I'm saying, 'These guys have guns, for God's sake, give him the damn wings before they kill us.' And he said, 'They're not getting my wings,' so I repeated, 'Don't be so damn stubborn, give him the damn wings!' And he wouldn't give him the wings and the guy backed off. But if this guy was in another frame of mind, you [*points to Earl*] wouldn't be here, and I wouldn't be here, and Sam wouldn't be here. He could have just shot us, and nobody asks questions, then. So that's where I met him.

Then they would collect us and we would go to central point, and they would ship you across the country to a place called Dusseldorf, which is an interrogation center. And they keep you there a few days while you get interrogated. And depending on what happened, they would send you to another place, until they got enough people together so they could try the freight train, or passenger train, or something, and then they send you off to your destination. That's how we all ended up in the same camp.

The camps were set up this way. If you were in the army or an infantryman, you were a prisoner of the German army. If you were in the navy and got picked up by the army some way or another, you are a prisoner of the navy. We were Air Corps people, so we were prisoners of the Luftwaffe, and I think we were treated better than anyone else. Because the British had so many Luftwaffe pilots in their camp, and Herman Goering would make sure the British would take care of his boys. We didn't have a picnic, it wasn't exactly the Hilton and it wasn't Hogan's Heroes, but we were much better off than anyone else in Germany. We got the same rations that [the guards] got, but they didn't really have all that much either, to tell you the truth. The German population, if you were a farmer you ate; if you lived in the city, you didn't get much either.

We didn't get much. We had Red Cross parcels come to us, but they kept saying, 'No parcels this week, your bombers hit three things—schools, hospitals, and supply trains with Red Cross parcels.' That's all our bombers ever hit. [Laughter]

The Red Cross parcels you are supposed to use to supplement rations they gave us, which was potatoes and soup and our lard or something. Everybody lost weight—I went from about 160 down to 129. They [points to Earl and Sam] would have to tell you what they lost, but most lost from 30 to 40 pounds. But we were still much better than those poor guys who ended up in Japan; there is no question about it. When they say, 'Geez, you were a prisoner of war, you had it tough,' I have kind of a guilty conscience because I knew guys that were in Japan.

Interviewer: Did you know any of the British troops or flyers in the PoW camps?

Sam, bombardier: We weren't up to their status; they didn't have anything to do with us.

Interviewer: They looked down on you?

Sam, bombardier: Oh yes, they looked down their noses on us.

Jerry, navigator: Can you say that again?

Interviewer: The British flyers, any contact with them or any conversations during the war?

Jerry, navigator: Well I got a chance to fly, not a mission but a practice. And I can't remember how it came about; we were talking about the other day. Some flew with us; it was sort of an exchange thing—they flew in and we talked to them.

I had great admiration for the Royal Air Force, they don't take the backseat to anybody. They had more guts when they were prisoners of war; if they could have had an [opportunity to] escape, they did. The British were taking the crème of the kids from the college, and putting them in the RAF. They were the crème de la crème. So when they got there, they had guys that could print, could forge, and could do this. They had engineers. You know, they could build tunnels, but they knew how to get air through it. When we got down to Moosburg, I see them with this little thing [*motions hands in a circular motion*]; they got a little blower with a duct going down there and you turn a few things on, and they had a red-hot flame going! The British had the ingenuity. I was watching this little thing, and I asked, 'What's that?' They devised all kinds of things— these guys were all experts in their own fields, and they knew how to forge documents, they knew how to do things with their time. They took uniforms and re-cut them and re-sewed them and made them into civilian clothes. And they got a hold of the train schedule and arrived at daylight out of the forest!

I can tell you another story about a PoW in our chapter who could speak seven languages. He was in our camp. He told me his name was Alex M.—about a year or two ago the Russian Ambassador gave him a medal down in Washington; it was in the papers. Now this guy was a prisoner in the camp that communicated with London. London dropped tons of cigarettes, which we used for currency. The Germans got a lot, but we got a lot in the camp. Alex got all of them; he had an apartment in Munich in which he was hiding, because he could speak the language; how the hell he got in and out of the camps, I have no idea. And he has Russians in this apartment, a whole story on its own, fantastic thing. [This is one of the ways] we got radio parts—cigarette companies sent tons and tons of cigarettes over. For every 5th or every 10th or every 100th carton or shipment, there was one pack, or in one cigarette, it had a part for a radio, and when it came we gave it to whomever we were supposed to give it to. Given enough of those, we'd get radios. We'd get cameras and we'd get parts and we'd sneak things in. So it was a very, very complicated thing.

Interviewer: Speaking of colonels, didn't you tell me that one time they dropped an officer, maybe a colonel, into your camp?

Earl, pilot: Yes, in our camp the colonel was running the camp. What was his name, the old fellow?

Sam, bombardier: He was a colonel in the B-24 group.

Earl, pilot: Yes.

Jerry, navigator: Once you were behind the barbed wire, the Germans said you were in the military organization, and the officers would run things, so that they don't have to. We have to tell our officers what we wanted. We had rules, very strict rules. You couldn't escape if you felt like it. You had to go to the escape committee, because you might do something to screw up somebody else's [escape plan], but anyways, let's not get into that yet.

In our compound, the west compound, there was a colonel. A fighter pilot, Jack Jenkins was his name, a Texan. He was the officer in charge. A story I knew about him is that he was standing outside when they have a roll call; they call it once at morning and once at night. They lined everybody up with space, and then two Germans go down and they count. They see that each line is complete and then they count up the lines [*counts in German*]. Then they count up this one and write it down, and add that one to make sure everybody is there. Well, that opens up a whole bunch of stories. However, this one particular day, we stand there, the counters are right; we were just standing there two hours. Something was said, and the colonel and the counting man came together, you know, and the next thing we know, they're standing there and there is a big argument. And the story as I got it was this—they said they wanted a list of all of the Jewish PoWs.[48] So the next day, we came out there and there's this big argument, there was raving and ranting. Jenkins says, 'That's it!' After all this standing around, we said, 'Well, what happened?' and the story filtered back. The German says, 'Give me a list of the names of the Jews!' Well, they all took the pledge that night, like they all had converted, like everybody was converted to Judaism. They would not give him the list of Jews! There was a 'hoo-ha' about it. The rumor was they wanted to take the Jews and hold them hostage up in the Alps. The next rumor that went around, I guess, maybe a month later, when they started to march a whole pack of us out. The story was they were going to take us as hostages to the Alps and use us as bargaining chips. Another story, which I've seen in print, one German general after the war said that Hitler had said he wanted all of the Allied airmen shot, because they

---

[48] *Jewish PoWs*- Jerry Silverman was Jewish.

were being coddled by Goering. We weren't, if you want to put this into perspective. Hitler said he wanted all the airmen shot [*pounds table with his fist for emphasis*], and they did not follow his orders. You know, we came this close [*gestures with his thumb and index finger very close together*], God-knows how many times. But that was one of the stories about Jack Jenkins, the fighter pilot from Texas. What made me cry was this is a guy from Texas, and even if he didn't like blacks, or he didn't like Jews, or Catholics, or whoever, no German was going to tell him what to do—no general was pushing him around! He says, 'We are Americans in this camp, and we are all the same.' There was another PoW camp for Allied officers in the North Sea, and a colonel was the head of a fighter group. The same thing happened up there. They asked him for a list of all Jews, and he said, 'You're not going to get it—if you're going to shoot them, you're going to shoot us all, because we are not going to tell you which ones to pick out.' So these are the things that make me feel damn proud to be an American.

Earl, pilot: I saw this colonel stand up to a German general. Prisoners were tearing the boards off the building down there in Nuremberg. A general came in there and says, 'The man who tears the next board off, we are just going to shoot him.' And the colonel just stuck his chest out: 'Anytime you want to start, start with me!' He had been on the march with us, but they had him in a wagon because he couldn't walk. And he was screaming at them back there because the Germans wouldn't let him up front with his troops. He was the same one that was at Sagan.

Jerry, navigator, to interviewer: 'Sagan' is Stalag Luft III—'Stalag' is 'prison camp,' 'Luft' is 'air,' 'Three,' it was the third one, and Sagan was a village nearby. [*To Earl*] Was he the fellow that wrote a letter about the bad conditions in the camp?

Sam, bombardier: Colonel Davenport?

Earl, pilot: Yes.

Sam, bombardier: I have it at home; it's twelve pages.

Earl, pilot: He wrote a letter on the conditions and slipped it to the Red Cross. And it went through.

Interviewer: Why were you tearing boards off the buildings?

Sam, bombardier: Heat. That was our heat.

Earl, pilot: Yes, we didn't have any other.

Sam, bombardier: Burned anything that would burn; we were freezing.

Earl, pilot: Yes, that same night, you could hear the boards being torn off.

Jerry, navigator: This was in Nuremberg.

Earl, pilot: Yes.

Earl, pilot: In Sagan we were using boards to make the tunnels.

Sam, bombardier: We were taking the boards off to make tunnels.

Earl, pilot: We were taking the bed stakes out of the beds.

Jerry, navigator: Next thing you know you were sleeping on three boards.

Interviewer: For escape?

Earl, pilot: Yes.

Sam, bombardier: That is when they were digging the tunnels.

Earl, pilot: So I was saying, you see, you had to shore up for every inch you made.

Sam, bombardier: And when the guys touched down straight so many feet, they had to shore it up with the wood. Then they'd start this way [*motions with hands*], and every time they'd move they'd have to shore it up. They made a gadget that they had to carry the dirt. They made a rope that they put wheels on. The guy had only room to go through. He could not turn around, you see. When he came out, he had to come out backwards.

Earl, pilot: At first they had to bring the dirt out in stockings, but they had gardens, see. They'd mix the dirt in with that [out in the garden]. Well, then the Germans stopped the gardening business.

So then they figured it out and we had a whole bunch of people go out in the field and drop the dirt.

Jerry, navigator: [*stands up, points just below the knee, walks around, demonstrating*] The stocking is right on his leg, tied with a string, and you walked out and pulled the string. But the dirt is going to look different; so they put a little out, then they walk, and mix a little up… They claim that the field there was raised six inches! The Germans drove a tank, and a little would collapse and we would have to dig deeper.

Earl, pilot: That happened when they brought a load of potatoes in Sagan, and about three days later, before they came and checked it. In the first camp that we were in north of Berlin.

The German soldiers were not supposed to think for themselves, and they drove across this tunnel, it caved in, so they got another wagon and unloaded that one and moved it on out. Then the officers came and spotted it, and of course I heard this story from other guys in there, because I'm not privileged to everything, but by then our tracks were all covered up and they didn't know anything about tunnels.

Jerry, navigator: Let me tell you about the escape committee. Every prisoner of war was expected to escape at all times—the reason being you tie up more German troops guarding you, it keeps them away from the lines—but if everyone tried to escape at once, it would mess up the other guy. So if you wanted to get out, they would help you, but you needed a plan to get over the fence. Once you got over the fence, they would get you clothes, timetables for trains, tickets, you know, maps, the whole bit. They could get you this stuff, but you had to go to the escape committee.

Let's say [a guy] wants to escape and has a plan. The committee would review it, and say, 'Okay, go, we will try it such and such night,' then they will try to find the weather report, for good cover. Two or three days before his plan of escape, somebody goes out of the barracks at night, and they clip some wires and make some tracks, and return. The Germans get up in the morning and they see this, they count, you know, and [they think] one guy is missing! But he's not missing—I'm up in the attic somewhere [*points to the ceiling*]! So then they line everybody up and you go through, past the desk, and they check your number and your picture and identify you and say, 'Silverman is missing.' That's the guy we're looking for, but I'm up in the attic. Three days later, one of the guys planning to escape goes out in the honey wagon[49] or potato wagon or to the hospital, and he gets out. Now I come down from the ladder, or the attic, and I'm standing where I'm supposed to stand; it doesn't make any difference—they don't know he's gone, you see? They're still looking for me! So until he goofs and gets caught on the outside, he is still free. This is why they had an escape committee. You know, just an example of how they did things.

Interviewer: You had to organize it.

Earl, pilot: And you did not try to escape on your own. It had to be approved by the committee.

Interviewer: Now how many men were on the committee? Were there officers?

Jerry, navigator: One guy was called 'Big X.' I don't know who he was; he was number one. His assistant was called 'Little X,' and I think you can find that in the movie *The Great Escape*, what went on in that camp. It was only across the wire from where we were in the next camp. We had towers there, they were the guards: all Germans were called 'goons'—so they called them 'goon boxes.' And there were little wires about this high [*motions about six inches with his hands*] called a 'warning wire,' and if you stepped over it, you were shot. If you were playing ball and the ball goes over, you wave to

---

[49] *honey wagon*- a cart or vehicle for carrying human excreta to dump or distribute elsewhere

the guard and point. You'd hop and if you pick up the ball and went back, it was okay, but if you go the other way, they'd start shooting. Then there was a barbed wire fence; it was a big fence, and then there was another fence. Between these two fences there were German Shepherds running around, you know, walking back and forth in case anybody went through. Also between the fences there were goon boxes up there. They had German guards we called 'ferrets'.[50] The barracks were put on the blocks, so that they could see through, go underneath, so you couldn't dig a tunnel, theoretically. There were always people standing around, saying, 'Goon up!' You know, that meant if you're doing anything, put it away, there's a German in the area; they might walk through the place, they might go under, they might hang around, they might listen, so consequently, with the American sense of humor, funny incidents would take place. I didn't see this, but I heard about it. Every [barracks] had twelve guys with pails; each guy had a pail of water. One day one of these ferrets would go underneath [the barracks crawlspace] and start snooping around, and they'd say, 'Okay, fellas, let's do it today!' They'd go down with scrubbing brushes—'Scrub your floors, men!' —and on the command, '1-2-3,' everybody would dump their buckets, and this wet rat comes out yelling. 'Oh, so sorry, Hans, we didn't know.' [*Laughs; Earl and Sam chuckle*]

Interviewer: Where would the tunnels be?

Jerry, navigator: They had ways of getting tunnels. They would dummy up things, latrines or...

Sam, bombardier: They took the stove. Remember the stove?

Jerry, navigator: I can't ever get how they linked the stove down to the tunnel below. They went through the stove, probably through the space, and then they'd have a pallet of some sort covering the tunnel, which they would cover with dirt. There must have

---

[50] *German guards we called 'ferrets'*-special anti-escape guards

been some way to get through this stove and get underneath their building. They'd lift this thing up and start digging their tunnels.

Earl, pilot: See, at first, the building sat on the ground and everybody was digging. It was later that they [built them] up on stilts. In the washroom, it was concrete, so I think the one in the *Great Escape,* they went down through the manholes in the bathrooms.

Jerry, navigator: They had three tunnels: Tom, Dick, and Harry. I remember that.

*

The March

Over a quarter million Allied prisoners were under German control by 1945. Between January and April, in a scene to be played out all over the Reich, hundreds of thousands of slave laborers, concentration camp victims, and PoWs were force-marched out of their camps to other locations to escape being liberated by the advancing Russian and western Allied powers. On January 27, Hitler himself ordered the captured airmen out of Stalag Luft III to camps west of Berlin.[17] On the same day, Soviet forces overran Auschwitz death camp, less than 250 miles to the southeast; the Russians were also closing in hard less than a hundred miles away to the north and south of the PoW camp. With little, the men shuffled out into the cold and snow towards Bavaria. The rumor mill had it that they were going to be executed or simply marched to death, on Hitler's orders, or that they were going to be held as bargaining chip hostages in the Bavarian Alps, where the SS planned to make a last stand.

Some of these forced marches indeed lasted for weeks in some of the harshest winter conditions of the 20th century. Men fell ill with typhus and dysentery, often contracted by resting in the same places along the march.[18] Many men died from exposure and hunger; some were beaten to death when they fell, while in other situations, guards found themselves little better off than the prisoners they were to guard, as time went on. Some townspeople, fearful of the Russian advance, gave assistance to them, while others angrily pelted the prisoners with rocks and debris as they wearily shuffled into a new town.

Interviewer to Earl, pilot: You said you thought you had the best crew over there. Do you still think that?

Earl, pilot: Yes.

Jerry, navigator: Who said that?

Earl, pilot: Me.

Sam, bombardier: And I second that.

Jerry, navigator: [*joking*] And who gave you the authority?

Sam, bombardier: [*pointing to Earl*] Him.

Interviewer: [*pointing to Sam*] Is this the bombardier who had the amnesia?

Earl, pilot: Yes.

Interviewer: After you were shot down?

Earl, pilot: This was on the forced march.

Jerry, navigator: To this day he's got amnesia. [*Laughter*]

Earl, pilot: [*pointing to Jerry*] He was on the march, too. There were about 10,000 of us on the march.

Interviewer: What about the forced march?

Earl, pilot: Well, they have heard my version of it, let someone else give them their version of it.

Sam, bombardier: Well, this is in January 1945. The Germans didn't want us to be liberated in any way, shape, or form, so they were moving us all, going west through the forest.

Interviewer: Because they wanted you as bargaining chips.

Jerry, navigator: Well, that's the rumor; the prisoner of war camps are the greatest rumor factories in the world.

Interviewer: Sure, you don't have any information.

Sam, bombardier: Well, we did have good information.

Earl, pilot: We had a radio.

Sam, bombardier: Yes, we had a radio; the Germans could never find it.

Earl, pilot: They would ask, when we were moving, 'Taking your radio with you?'

Interviewer: Where did you hide it?

Sam, bombardier: You took it apart and put it together: everybody had a little piece.

Jerry, navigator: In our camp, it was in an accordion. I always heard about it, then a book got published ... and in it they had the picture of the accordion and I start jumping up and down like a ma- niac. I said, 'By God, I heard about that thing!' and here it is, there is a picture of it. The guys are sitting around and the Germans are taking everything apart, and one guy is sitting there playing 'Home on the Range,' and the radio is inside the accordion that this guy is playing.

Earl, pilot: And the BBC[51] knew it too, because they beamed stuff to us.

Sam, bombardier: We used to have a map on the wall, this big map the guys have drawn, and we knew where everyone [invading ar- mies] was in the war. Where the French were moving up, where the Russians were, where the Germans were. They used to come to us to look at our map to find out what the hell was going on. But the radio always picked up from outside, always like a newscast. And there it was, we would have it.

Earl, pilot: And on that same map, it would have our line where we knew it was, marked. Then we would have their line where they advertised marked, and they didn't agree at all.

Jerry, navigator: In many cases they agreed, but the interesting part was we would get interpreters and we would get the German news. And, of course, we would get our own news from the BBC,

---

[51] *BBC*- British Broadcasting Corporation

and the Germans would say that, 'All victorious troops strongly defended this particular town,' then the next day, 'All victorious and
glorious and loyal Nazi troops successfully beat down two platoons
of American infantry at this town.' But now they were back over
here! The next day they beat the hell out of us over here, and then
they beat the hell out of us over here, then over there. When we
look at the map, we laugh at the thing, but they haven't won a battle
and they are slowly losing the war.

Sam, bombardier: They're backing up and backing up. Funny how
they came in one day and said, 'Everybody get packed because we
are going to move out!' So everybody starts packing and it started
to snow in the afternoon. It was more like flurries and there was
probably only an inch of snow on the ground, but as it got later in
the day, the snow got heavier. And we had to go, so when we left
there the snow was about four inches deep, when we went out.

Jerry, navigator: Middle of the night, midnight.

Sam, bombardier: And everybody has their sack, everything they
could carry.

Earl, pilot: We really didn't have any idea where we were going,
or anything.

Sam, bombardier: We were back six to eight buildings from the
front, and as we went along, we could see where guys would be
dumping stuff along the side of the road: they took extra food, we
had a warehouse for canned food, and they were taking the sugar.
Because while you were walking you wanted energy, so you would
eat the sugar. So I packed, I would say, probably 200 cubes of sugar
in my pockets, and that is what I ate as I went along.

We walked and walked, and I found it getting cold, and everybody is getting tired, and we keep going. It's like five, six, seven
o'clock in the morning. It's getting colder out. I had a scarf around
my face and it was just a ball of ice; I would have to reach up and
break it so I could get air to my face. My feet were frozen.

Interviewer: How many hours had you been walking?

Jerry, navigator: About three days, [at that point].

Sam, bombardier: And you never got warm, we just kept going and going, we couldn't even change socks if you wanted to, so we had wet socks in cold weather—so as far as I'm concerned, that's what happened to me.

The next day we marched almost twenty-some hours, so now we were coming up to some town, now everybody is falling over. Then I did something that I didn't even know I did. I was in a group where everybody made a pledge to watch each other. I found myself off the side of the road and I lay in the snow and I said to myself, 'Wow, this is so warm.' I was so damn cold, I could hardly do anything. In the meantime, when I lay over, some guys saw me—one was a captain and one was a major—they saw me walk over and lie down, and they grabbed me. They stood me up and shook me, they asked me questions, and I—I didn't know anything, so they picked me up and made me walk. We got to this town and that's when he [*points to Earl*] came around; he was looking for me and he was hollering my name.

I was standing there and he comes over to me: 'Sam.' And I knew: 'You're Earl, you're the pilot.' When they had questioned me, I didn't know my name or anything, or where I lived—I was gone! The only thing I knew was [*points to Earl*]: 'You're Earl, you're the best goddamn pilot in the whole Air Force.'

Interviewer: Well, how many days had you been there?

Sam, bombardier: Well, that was after some 20 hours, we froze walking.

Earl, pilot: I went right to him [at that point]. I had gone through the same procedure as Sam—I actually sat down in the snow and they came to me... so I got up and I moved again. At about this time they're yelling, 'Sam Lisica,' and I woke up and got hold of him; I was all right by then. When you see someone worse than you are... I kept him moving then.

Sam, bombardier: When I started getting all mixed up, I do remember I knew I was walking fast, but I guess there were five, six, or seven barracks [of men in our group]. We went out in barracks, so everybody stays together—[but then] I walked through these guys, and all of a sudden, I'm the leader. I'm out in front of everybody, and that's how they saw me take off to the side of the road [to lie down].

Interviewer: How many people would be on this march?

Jerry, navigator: From the camp...

Earl, pilot: They estimated about ten thousand, didn't they?

Jerry, navigator: Stalag Luft III had a north compound, a south compound, a west and an east compound: we were in the west, this was the newest one. The north compound was the one that was all British, and that's where the famous *Great Escape* occurred: where they all went through a tunnel and 50 of them were caught and were murdered.

Jerry, navigator: And I guess three guys made it to, I think, Sweden: they made a movie out of that, Steve McQueen, there's another movie coming out about the same compound we were in. Bruce Willis is in it, which is going to be interesting, because nobody in the place was as old as Bruce Willis is right now.[52] [*Laughter*]

But anyway, when they took us out, one of the compounds went directly from there all the way to a place called Moosburg. The rest of us went on the march we were on, about a week, a week and a half, we took stops—we had no idea, no recollection of them. We eventually marched for about three days to the next town, we were going to stop—the next town, it was bitter cold. They kept us in a church one night, on marble floors. If you want to freeze to death,

---

[52] *as old as Bruce Willis is right now*-actor in *Hart's War* (2002).

I'll tell you what, that's the place. Another ten would come out [die], and another two, you know.

Then, some miracle happened. They put us into a factory, it was a pottery factory, and the floors were warm, actually warm. All the time in Germany we never felt warm; we were always freezing to death, and they kept us there for three days! I'm thinking that's what saved a lot of our guys who would have died from pneumonia or whatever. We got our chance to get our strength back.

The pottery factory was worked by Polish and French slave laborers. In the basement were the kilns, which operated day and night, warming the floors above. This reprieve indeed saved many; by this point, the line of prisoners extended nearly 30 miles.[19]

From there they marched us a day or two, then they took us to a place called Spremberg, and they put us into boxcars, 55 to 60 guys in a boxcar. Which only really held 40 or 8, 40 men or eight horses. We had 50, 55, 60 men, depending, with only one little slit for everyone to look through. Everyone could not sit down at the same time, and we were trapped in this thing for about three days.

Interviewer: Was the train moving?

Sam, bombardier: Oh yes, they were taking us west.

Jerry, navigator: They were taking us down to Nuremberg. Then we would end up in a prison camp in Nuremberg.

Sam, bombardier: That's when we all had discipline.

Jerry, navigator: This was between the train ride and the marching. Then one thing, then another, and the train having to stop to wait for the German soldiers to move so the train could continue moving again; the rail lines were all plugged up. Our train was strafed, lucky for us but unlucky for the guys at the other end—they were hit by our own P-47s. The Germans did not go through the trouble of putting red crosses on the trains with prisoners, but they did on their own troop trains.

The remnants of the Volkssturm[53] were still streaming eastward in a futile effort to stem the tide of the Soviet advance, clogging the roads and railways as masses of humanity surged past them in a desperate attempt to outrun the Russians. At Spremberg, near the beginning of February, the men were finally issued some black bread, having walked over sixty miles in five days.[20] Then they were crowded into the boxcars, where many of the men suffered indignities again in freezing temperatures.

Sam, bombardier: Then we all got dysentery. They stopped one time, and everybody had to go, and they would open the door. Everybody would run out, sitting by the railroad track...

Jerry, navigator: I've been waiting for years to hear from somebody of one of the funniest things I saw in the war. There were so many of us out of the train at one time, and we were on this track. The train was standing still, a bright, sun-shining day, the German guards were in the field with their guns and everything, and the guys came out to relieve themselves. About 150 guys sitting there with their pants down, all sitting straight, mooning the guards. [*Laughter*]

Sam, bombardier: When you've got dysentery, you could knock a fly dead from 50 paces because all the pressure and water and— zoom! The best part was when we were done, we would come walking by and they would say nothing to us. [*Laughter*]

The men arrived at Stalag XIIID at Nuremberg, an area that was a favorite target of their previous bombing raids due to its location near the railroad marshalling yards. Conditions here were abysmal, with rotten and vermin-infested food.

Jerry, navigator: You talk about the American sense of humor, if it wasn't for the American sense of humor... We always had funny

---

[53] *Volkssturm*-the national militia, composed of units of conscripts between age 16 and 60.

names for people; you could always find a funny moment. There was an air raid and one of our own bomb group came at us; they were dropping bombs around Nuremberg, and turning away, but one plane didn't, and it was coming straight at us! I did see this happen—some [American] guy grabbed hold of a guard and started shaking him, yelling, 'Where's the Luftwaffe, where's the Luftwaffe!' [*Laughter*]

Interviewer: And he was an American?

All: Yes.

Sam, bombardier: He told him to take out that bomber so it would not drop bombs on us! [*Laughter*]

Sam, speaking to Earl: Do you remember the day we were marching, we pulled off of the march and into the farmhouse, and we went up and knocked on the door? We asked them if we could wash our faces and shave, because me, I was taking a shave every day—no matter where I was, I shaved.

Jerry, navigator: I always shaved.

Sam, bombardier: So anyhow, you talked sign language and whatever you thought you knew in German, until you strike a deal. And then she says, 'Okay, wash up.' Their stoves were big cast iron stoves and on their sides they had water tanks, so they were cooking over here [*points to the right*], and the water stayed hot all the time. So they'd just pick up the lid, dunk the cup in, and give us a bucket of hot water. She said, 'Go out behind the barn, and there's a wash basin and a mirror.' And she even gave us towels. And she had two little kids, and we went out there and we got washed and came back and brought the stuff back. We came in, and there were four plates. We had fried bacon, fresh eggs, and she had just finished making rye bread in the oven. That was the breakfast I got on that march, the four of us got. So, anyhow, we said, what the hell can we give her? I had some leftover sugar cubes in my pocket, and I had a couple pieces of candy, and she had these little kids. We were talking, and all of a sudden, we made sense to each other. She was saying she was a widow, her husband was killed on the eastern front, and she had these kids and I think she had her mother living with her on this farm. I don't know how they worked it, but anyhow, we sat down and we gave her this and that, but she didn't want it. Anyhow, we got up to leave, and she turned to each of us—we were in our 20s and she was probably about 47 years old. She came over to us and gave us a big hug and said, 'Good luck.'

Interviewer: Now, is this after the war ended?

Sam, bombardier: That's when we were prisoners and we were marching from...

Earl, pilot: From Nuremberg to Moosburg...

Interviewer: How could you do that? Would the Germans let you do that?

Earl, pilot: We actually were bribing the guards to stay with us, because there were SS troops in the area—and a bunch of Americans walking without guards, you'd have problems. But now, along the same line, I didn't get into a deal that you got into [*points to Sam*]. I got into a store that a couple of ladies were running. They let about 15 or 16 of us in there and locked the door, and the guards pulled the shade. And the guards were outside beating on the door trying to get in. She let us get what we wanted and she'd sneak us out the back door.

You see, this was at the end, and I actually saw three women converge on the commandant of the camp. A big old fat major, he was at Sagan, then he was down in Nuremberg, and he was riding a bicycle on that march. I saw three women, two of them from each side and one of them from in the front, caught him on his bicycle and dumped him right out there in front of all of us. And then all the civilians wanted to know when the Americans were going to get there. Because, see, the Russians were coming too. They just wanted Americans. All the civilians, by then, on that march, they were with us. They wanted us there; they wanted the Americans there before the Russians got there.

Jerry, navigator: I told this story yesterday. I did eventually about 10 years ago meet one of the guys who was in this room with me, and he remembered everything as I did, because sometimes you think, 'I'm not sure if this happened or I heard it or what.' But this is what happened. It was on my birthday, the night before was a Saturday. They put us in a barn and made a big fuss about all these displaced workers, and they told these girls they were to fix up beds for us. So they made hay and got a blanket, you know, they took care of us and that was nice. But the next day he invited us into his kitchen. We came into the kitchen, large kitchen, larger than this room, and they cooked over in that area and the family sat there. We sat at a table for six over here [*pointing about the room*], so I had mixed emotions about this, which I'll tell you about at the end. They gave us pigs' knuckles, they boiled potatoes, and after the meal we sat at the table and he came over with a pad and said, 'I would like you to write a note to your commanding officer of the unit that occupies this area.' This would introduce 'Herr So and So,' who's the burgermeister, the mayor of the village here, and 'that he had the six of you there, treated you well, gave you breakfast, took care of you, and gave you good quarters, clean quarters in the barn, and kept you warm.' Because it was April—April 15 was my birthday, so it's etched—it was a Sunday, and he asked us if anybody was Catholic, and if we wanted to go to church with the family and so on. And they didn't go, and I said, 'I'm not signing anything like that.' The reason I didn't want to sign was because I remembered when they were winning in 1941, 1942, it was all, 'Our boys, our boys,' and I didn't see anybody say, 'Oh, this is terrible!' They were cheering, you know? Now that they were losing all of a sudden they turned their faces around. So I said, 'I'm not signing it.' Another guy said, 'I'm not signing it.' And then one guy said, 'Let me write it. I'll write it.' He got annoyed at the mayor, so he said, 'Let me write it.' So he writes it, and this is what he wrote: 'To the commanding officer...' And then he added one more part, and said, 'Please do the undersigned a favor and *take care* of this guy,' and then he signed it.

Sam, bombardier: 'Take care' meant different than take care of your welfare.

Jerry, navigator: What does it mean to an American? 'Take care of this guy.' So I've often wondered. I'd like to go back to find out whatever happened to him.

Earl, pilot: See, that's the only thing that really bothered me when I got back. On the march we had in January, the civilian crowd, they weren't with us at all, and then in April, boy, between January and April, they were going from this way to that way [*points from left to right*].

*

Liberation

Interviewer: Do you remember if you were liberated on the same day?

Earl, pilot: Yes; we were in the same camp, but we didn't all get out on the same date.

Interviewer: That was when General [George S.] Patton came through?

Sam, bombardier: He came in on his tank with his pearl-handled pistols; they were .38s he wore on his waist.

Interviewer: Did you all see him?

All: Yes.

Sam, bombardier: There were supposed to be 100,000 to 120,000 people in this camp at a time and they had other nationalities. They had Russians, they had Greeks, and they had Italians. I know they had a lot of Italians. The main gate was over here, and there was an abbey and there were buildings like this [*motioning with his hand*], and there was another gate and the Canadians were in there. The first thing we knew, our planes were coming overhead. One of the great experiences I remember now, and I hope these guys remember, two fighter planes with their contrails were making a great big '8' in the sky [*motioning in the air*], and the other one made a '9' for the Ninth Air Force, and [*motions with arm raised in air*] that's our boys! I mean, they were sharp! A P-51 would come by like this, you know, and we'd cheer and the Germans would get upset.

Anyway, we heard small arms fire one day. Now I'm air crew; I don't know anything about small arms. But when I see dirt hopping around, I figure something's up, so we scooted! And there was a battle; you could hear 'crackity-crack.' That's what I remember, and the next thing, people are looking out, and someone said, 'Look down there at the main gate!', and the American flag was flying and we went berserk, we just went berserk! We were looking at the goon tower and there's no goons there, there are Americans up there! And we saw the American flag, I mean—to this day I start to well up when I see the flag… [*Gets emotional*]

About three days later, word came that Patton was coming in, so by this time you could go from one compound to the other. I was on a roof peak of a building; there were only about six or eight of us, [but guys on rooftops all over]… there were French on that side, Canadians on this side [*motioning with his hands*]. Here comes this flying wedge of tanks, and here's General Patton, with his chest breaking the ice because he's like the icebreaker! And I'd known of him since Pearl Harbor—he's got these pearl-handled guns, so he's walking through, and the British salute, and we heard a French guy say, 'Mon General,' and there's an American next to us who says, 'Hey, Georgie, where the hell have you been, what took you so long?' He used an expletive that I'm not going to use: 'Where the bleep have you been?' George Patton, the first guy he acknowledged, was him! [*points at Earl, who laughs*] That's my memory of

George Patton. You can say what you want about George Patton; he liberated me, that's my boy.

Interviewer: So that was the beginning of May?

Sam, bombardier: That was April 29, 1945, a date that is etched in my memory.

Interviewer: You got a salute out of him, Earl?

Earl, pilot: Yes! See, these guys were more mobile than me; I had this bad knee and I wasn't getting around too fast, but I got up and ducked around the building, and there he was! I threw a salute at him, and he returned it; I just happened to be there all by myself, coming around that building. And he was upset. He said, 'You guys are all officers, and this is what they did to you?' Patton didn't hang around long; he made his little speech and he was gone.

Sam, bombardier: They sent up a field station, and we hadn't had nothing good to eat for months and...

Earl, pilot: Bread would look like angel food cakes, it was so white. We were used to that 'sawdust' bread.

Sam, bombardier: But the best thing was the Russian prisoners; they left the camp, they went out and killed some cows [and brought them back] on their shoulders; 'Gonna roast some beef!'

Jerry, navigator: That's right...

Earl, pilot. They got [food] from the guards, too...

Sam, bombardier: And they made the guards scared. So they went to the railroad yard and broke into a boxcar; they found condensed milk in gallon cans. And the Russians brought them to us in our tent where I was staying. They brought us the condensed milk and the army started to deliver the bread, and we looked at that bread and we were afraid; it looked so good, it looked like angel food cake. Everyone just looked at it, then we started eating it; we put the condensed milk on it. Then they started making food and we got good food. There must have been 50 guys in our tent.

Jerry, navigator: We had big white tents, far more than 50 guys...

Sam, bombardier: Great big tents, circus tents…

Earl, pilot: We had hay to lie on, clean hay, so it wasn't like back in Nuremberg; boy, Nuremberg was horrible…

Jerry, navigator: One thing about the Russians cobbling up the livestock was that the farmers got a hold of some American officer, because the Russians were killing off all the sheep. And they'd just cut off a couple steaks they wanted, and discard the rest of it, and then they'd move along. So he said, 'We're going to need this food, to feed you guys and us, our people.' But by the time he convinced this particular officer [to try to prevent the wanton slaughter of his animals], the farmer came back and said, 'Forget it!' [*waves his hand*]. His herd had been wiped out.

We spoke with some Russians who had some broken German, and Russians with some of our Polish guys, you know, we had sort of communications with them. At this point, we were at this [airfield], a German fighter base, and we were waiting for C-47s to come and get us. We hung around and exchanged some stories; we would tell the Russians how we were getting out of this, and ask, 'Incidentally, how are you guys getting out of this?' They said, 'We are walking home, we walk to Turkistan.' That name sticks in my mind, 1,200 or 1,400 miles, and me and the other fellows, we asked, 'Well, aren't they coming to get you, so you can go home by truck, or fly home?' Now that the war was over, Moscow didn't give a damn about them, and if they were going to go home, they were going to have to get out on their own [*motions with thumb, as in hitching a ride*]. They said, 'They do not recognize that we were prisoners of war—we were written off as dead, we were supposed to die.' You know, 'We either go forward or die, we cannot go back.' That's what they were up against.

*

'Thank God every day'

Jerry, navigator: I say that any person today, or any kid today who's growing up, should get on his hands and knees every night and thank God that he was born in the United States of America. Because even today you could be born in Africa, you have a fifty-fifty chance of getting to be twelve years old. You have AIDS all over, you've got one group murdering the other, you know, within their own country, killing each other, and all the while this is going on and on... in Israel, Syria, and Lebanon, and such. I mean, you can't even go to school without being afraid your bus is going to be machine-gunned or blown up. And people that live in this country have no idea how lucky they are.

In Mexico they're having a terrible time. They're coming by the droves to come over here and work. Same thing with the Canadians, they should be damn glad and thank God every day that they were born in that country. And I don't think anybody knows it! There's a quote by George Santayana, and it's posted at the Air Force Museum, and I can't recite it verbatim but it says, 'Those who do not learn from history are condemned to relive it,' to live it again—and nobody knows!

We spoke about this the other day [*pointing to Earl*], you know, they want the Olympics in China, and the pros say, 'Well, you know, we'll get in there and we'll do good, and they'll realize that they have to become more democratic.' And it can't be that way with their people, we don't learn from history—in 1936 they held the Olympics in Munich, now didn't that make Hitler the nice guy? Imagine what he would have been if they didn't have the Olympics, how bad it could have been?

Everybody is worried about himself and nobody is worried about the United States. Nobody is worried about his or her country. They want their vans, their boats; they want their summer cottage, you know? They want their retirement plan, you know; they want 'theirs.'

Sam, bombardier: It makes you laugh.

Jerry, navigator: In the meantime this stuff is using up gas and oil. You know, there's only so much juice in an orange, and there's only so much oil. Now, where is the oil right now that's being used up? Arabia? They want to take off a few yards of oil up here and some in the U.S. When this is done, who's going to have the oil? Russia, China, and India! [*To Earl and Sam*] So, boys, plan ahead! [*Chuckles*]

Sam, bombardier: We don't have anything to worry about. We're not going to be here.

Earl, pilot: Yes, well, you worry a little bit about your kids and grandkids.

Jerry, navigator: What you get out of the prisoner of war experience, it's amazing—I haven't seen this guy for 50 years [*points to Sam*], and politically, economically, and everything else, we're like twins. And you see any [former PoW]—that's why it broke my heart when John McCain dropped out [of the 2000 presidential race], because the guy is a former PoW. And I know—when you're a PoW, you suddenly realize what's important and what's not important. That's one thing you find out. The next important thing is that we've got to take care of this country first, and nobody seems to be giving a damn.

Interviewer: Have any of you been back to Germany since the war?

Sam, bombardier: Not me.

Jerry, navigator: They have tours—'do you want to go to the old prison camps,' you know, that's hot stuff. [*Sarcastically*] I get out of Sing-Sing[54]—after 15 years, do you think I'm going to go back and take a tour of the place? [*Laughter*]

Interviewer: So you have no desire to retrace those steps?

---

[54] *Sing-Sing*- a maximum security prison in New York State.

Sam, bombardier: I wanted to go to just let my wife see England and France, but she'd get sick. You know? So, I can't do nothing, I was lucky to get here.

Interviewer: So what about German people today? Do you know any? Do you have any desire to know any?

Sam, bombardier: The men that I knew were the civilians, the ones who were left behind. We got to talk to them and I thought most of them I met were pretty nice people.

Jerry, navigator: I can tell you a story about that. If you're old enough, you have a story for everything.

I used to be in the driving school business. When I first got in, I worked for the summer and took it as a temporary job, and I was teaching a woman by the name of Katie G. She was a German woman, and also a nice woman. I just didn't get around to telling her that I had bombed Germany, you know, my job was to teach her how to drive. And she was married to Max. And Max is a salesman for a German company that makes hardware for operating, such as scissors, scalpels, etc. And in the course of discussion with him, it turned out that he was a German fighter pilot. We started to compare notes, and probably, we were mixed up, and we were flying every day, so he must have been flying when I was there, because he was flying in that period of time, and he was in an Me-109. Now this is the nicest guy in the world, I mean, we got along very well. They invited my wife and me, we went over, had dinner there, they wanted something done to their building and our scout master was a contractor, so I fixed it up with the scout master and he got the job. She was a chief housekeeper in a hospital in Hempstead [Long Island] nearby, and whenever anyone was in the hospital that I knew, I'd go in and see them, and then go down and see Katie. Katie saw to it that they got a little extra of this and that, that kind of thing. They were the nicest people in the world. Here's a guy doing his job for his country, I'm a guy doing my job, we were trying to kill each other, and 30, 40 years later, I don't see anything wrong with this guy.

But I'm not judging the German people or the German frame of mind; I'm judging Max G., individual. Now, I'm Jewish, and this guy's Luftwaffe, and he was fighting for the Nazis. He should have said to his wife, 'What? You let him teach you to drive?' Never happened. I taught Arabs, by the way, and if they pass, they think you're the greatest instructor in the world. If they fail, you're a bum. [*Laughter*] So anyway, they're passing and I'm getting a lot of these Arab people, and I'm getting them from Lebanon, I'm getting them from Syria, and I'm getting them from Israel itself, they're Palestinian Arabs. So one day I asked one guy, his name was Habeeb, I said, 'You guys know I'm Jewish. With all of this that's going on in Palestine, how come you're using me?'

And he said, 'That's Palestine, this is here. You're a good teacher; we want you.'

So if you go on a person-to-person level—and I've taught people in that area from all over—everybody wants the same thing. They want a good job, they want a clean house, they want a roof that doesn't leak, they want their bellies full, they want their kids clean, behaved, kept out of trouble, they want their kids educated, they want to enjoy Jones Beach just like everyone else, on a person-to-person basis. But when you get a rabble rouser that whips up the crowd [*waves hand in the air*], you know, I could mention a few of ours right now, whenever they set up a camera, bingo!—they are there. I'm not going to mention any names, you know who I'm talking about...

Some of the things that shake you—my younger son, I used to look down on him, now he is looking over me. I've found the packet with my old record and ID and so on from about 1943. I was 5' 10 ½". I think I'm about five feet even right now!

Sam, bombardier: They say you shrink, gravity's pushing us down. My kids all called me 'Shorty'; their mother's short. They're all over six feet.

Jerry, navigator: I used to have three sons and a daughter, now I've got three fathers and a mother.

[*Interviewer laughs*]

Jerry, navigator: Your day will come, don't snicker, your day will come...

Sam Lisica passed away at age 85, five years after this roundtable interview. Jerry Silverman died at age 89 in 2008, two years after Sam. I invited Earl to my high school again in 2011, where I had the honor of introducing him to the granddaughter of his liberator, General George S. Patton.

Earl M. Morrow, World War II Memorial, Washington, D.C.,
June 2016. Photo: Jessica Morrow Brand.

Trails in the Sky

I waited on the tarmac as the crew prepared the airplane for takeoff. A high school friend had let me know that the B-17 was coming to town, and I was going up in it for a thirty-minute ride over Lake George, New York, the 'Queen of American Lakes.' I hurried to the airport and filled out the pre-flight paperwork, and was briefed along with seven others on the 'dos and don'ts' of a once-in-a-lifetime ride aboard an authentic World War II Flying Fortress.

Once inside the narrow midsection, we were strapped along the fold-up metal seats for takeoff. Passengers were advised to insert the orange earplugs provided, but as the engines spat and coughed to life, I left mine out. I wanted all of my senses intact for my time in the belly of the bird.

We were off, lumbering down the runway and into the air. Our cruising altitude was probably less than a thousand feet as we headed north, the shadow of the bird plain as day over the golf course greens. From the top turret position I looked back on French Mountain and the city of Glens Falls, the hub of the nationally recognized 'Hometown, USA' activity 75 years ago. Moments later, from the waist gun windows, I could see the waves and pleasure craft on Lake George only a few hundred feet below. We banked over the Sagamore Hotel and Resort in Bolton Landing, completing the 180-degree turn to return via the lake southward over Lake George Village. People on summer holiday looked up and waved; a friend dining on the lake texted to ask if I was aboard, but at the time I was too absorbed in my thoughts and my surroundings to look at the message.

I looked at my fellow passengers—a red-headed teenager, riding solo with his father's blessing, another man about my age, seemingly as absorbed as I had been, a younger touristy woman, jaws working furiously to process a wad of chewing gum as she snapped miles of cell phone video and photographs. Certainly it was an experience that was photo-worthy. I took a few shots myself, and somehow captured the essence of serenity upon an older woman's face as she gazed out of the left waist gun window, not looking down at the lake, but drifting through the sky. Was she trying to live the moment of a special somebody: a brother, a father, or perhaps even a late husband? I didn't speak to her, but her serene look spoke volumes to me. Here I was, nearing the end of my own career as a teacher, knowing full well that my old friends who had once braved the skies over Europe were leaving me. In one of the most destructive machines of war, this lady just radiated peace, a level of contentedness and gratitude and everything else that I noted in the faces of some of these grizzled veterans sitting down for the first time in front of the camera. And I think they knew it too, opening up as they did for their interviewers, both young and old, students and professionals. They had a story to tell, before it was too late.

*

I last saw my friend Earl a few weeks ago. His daughter got in touch to say she would be in town, so I drove over to the old farmhouse where he grew up, bringing him a copy of my recently released first *War in the Air* book, where he is also prominently featured. His wife passed away a few years back, his PoW friends are gone now as well, but after turning 96 he is still plugging along, one day at a time. He might not get around like he used to, but he was excited to hold the book in his hands, and as he thumbed through it, he pointed excitedly to the B-17s he once commanded in a world that seems so long ago.

*

How soon we forget.

Our World War II veterans gave us a nation that for all of its imperfections survives as a model for others, a lesson in what it means to stand together during the tough times, often against seemingly insurmountable odds, in spite of our differences or innate biases. It may help us to recall that democracy is not only very fragile, it is also hardly even out of the cradle in the backdrop of world history. But as a wise philosopher-historian once told me, what sets democracy apart from every other experiment in history—in its pure form and in theory—is its defense of minorities. That doesn't exist yet, but maybe this form of government needs to be protected, and nourished. And maybe this is what the airmen, Marines, sailors, soldiers, and merchant marines who participated in the greatest cataclysm in the history of the world were fighting for.

The world does not have to be united, and, in fact, it never has been and never will be. We argue and we disagree all of the time. That is as it is, and as it should be; it's even part of what the Allies were fighting against: a 'New World Order.' But when the chips are down, the actions of this generation remind us of who we are as a nation, what we aspired to and achieved not so long ago, together. And that should be celebrated, fêted, and honored, while our veterans are still with us, and long after the last one departs.

The Airmen featured in this book

Clarence W. Dart: After the war, Clarence Dart married and he and his wife raised a large family in Saratoga Springs, New York. He worked nearly four decades for the General Electric Company and was a reservist in the New York Air National Guard, retiring with the rank of lieutenant colonel. Mr. Dart was inducted into the New York State Veterans' Hall of Fame in 2011. He passed away on February 17, 2012, at the age of 91.[21]

John G. Weeks: Following his military service, John briefly flew for commercial airlines. He then started a long career in business, concluding as a consultant to businesses trying to avoid bankruptcy. He and his wife had four children, and in retirement, he founded a mushroom farm in Washington County, New York. He was involved in his church and many civic organizations. He passed away on October 21, 2015, at the age of 93.[22]

Richard Faulkner: Richard Faulkner married and raised three children, working as a mechanic and then for 35 years at New York State Electric and Gas Company as a lineman. He was a member of American Legion, 100th Bomb Group Association, and the Air Forces Escape & Evasion Society. He passed away at age 89 on August 29, 2014.[23]

George FitzGibbon: As a reserve officer, George FitzGibbon was recalled during the Korean War when they needed pilots. He and his wife raised three children. He retired from the Air Force in 1969 as a lieutenant colonel, the operations officer of the 41st Air Refueling Squadron at Griffiss Air Force base in New York. Later he settled in Binghamton, New York, serving as the chief pilot for New York State Electric & Gas. He passed away at the age of 93 on May 5, 2015.[24]

Charles Corea: Charlie settled back in his hometown and married, raising four children with his wife of 68 years before his death. He was active in many civic organizations, and retired in 1984 as owner and publisher of the East Rochester Shopping Guide. He passed away at the age of 92 on August 26, 2014.[25]

Earl M. Morrow: Earl Morrow was a career airline pilot for American Airlines. He and his wife retired to the family farm in Hartford, New York, after his career, where he volunteered to transport fellow veterans to the VA hospital in Albany and was a sought-after speaker in local schools and community events.

Sam Lisica: Sam Lisica married and returned to Pennsylvania, retiring after 40 years with the Pittsburgh Forgings Steel Company. He and his wife raised four children; Mr. Lisica passed away on October 11, 2006, at the age of 85.

Jerry Silverman: After the war, Jerry married and raised four children on Long Island, New York, and founded his own driving school, where he worked for 25 years. He was active in civic organizations and the Northport VA, where he served as a driver for disabled veterans. He was also an active member of the Nassau/Suffolk Chapter of the American Ex-Prisoners of War. He passed away on October 4, 2008, at the age of 89.[26]

****

IF YOU LIKED THIS BOOK, you'll love hearing more from the World War II generation in my other books. On the following pages you can see some samples, and I can let you know as soon as the new books are out and offer you exclusive discounts on some material. Just sign up at matthewrozellbooks.com

Some of my readers may like to know that all of my books are **directly available from the author, with collector's sets which can be autographed** in paperback and hardcover. They are popular gifts for that 'hard-to-buy-for' guy or gal on your list.

Visit my shop at matthewrozellbooks.com for details.

Thank you for reading!

I hope you found this book interesting and informative; I sure learned a lot researching and writing it. What follows are some descriptions of my other books.

Find them all at matthewrozellbooks.com.

The Things Our Fathers Saw: The Untold Stories of the World War II Generation from Hometown, USA-Voices of the Pacific Theater

Volume 1 of The Things Our Fathers Saw® series started with my first book on the oral history of the men and women who served in the Pacific Theater of the war. It's been designated as an Amazon 'Great On Kindle' non-fiction selection—you can download it and get 25% purchase price credit towards another qualifying ebook. An audio version is also available. The Amazon paperback version is almost always ON SALE and shipping is always free with Amazon Prime for all my books.

> *"The telephone rings on the hospital floor, and they tell you it is your mother, the phone call you have been dreading. You've lost part of your face to a Japanese sniper on Okinawa, and after many surgeries, the doctor has finally told you that at 19, you will never see again. The pain and shock is one thing. But now you have to tell her, from 5000 miles away."*

> *— "So I had a hard two months, I guess. I kept mostly to myself. I wouldn't talk to people. I tried to figure out what the hell I was going to do when I got home. How was I going to tell my mother this? You know what I mean?" — **WWII Marine veteran**

But you don't have to start with this book—I constructed them so that you can pick up any of the series books and start anywhere—but it's up to you.

The Things Our Fathers Saw—The Untold Stories of the World War II Generation-Volume II: War in the Air—From the Great Depression to Combat

Volume 2 in the series deal with the Air War in the European Theater of the war. I had a lot of friends in the heavy bombers; they tell you all about what it was like to grow up during the Great Depression as the clouds of war gathered, going off to the service, and into the skies over Europe, sharing stories of both funny and heartbreaking, and all riveting and intense.

> — *"I spent a lot of time in hospitals. I had a lot of trouble reconciling how my mother died [of a cerebral hemorrhage] from the telegram she opened, announcing I was [shot down and] 'missing in action.' I didn't explain to her the fact that 'missing in action' is not necessarily 'killed in action.' You know? I didn't even think about that. How do you think you feel when you find out you killed your mother?"* —**B-24 bombardier**

> — *"I was in the hospital with a flak wound. The next mission, the entire crew was killed. The thing that haunts me is that I can't put a face to the guy who was a replacement. He was an eighteen-year-old Jewish kid named Henry Vogelstein from Brooklyn. It was his first and last mission. He made his only mission with a crew of strangers."* —**B-24 navigator**

> — *"The German fighters picked us. I told the guys, 'Keep your eyes open, we are about to be hit!' I saw about six or eight feet go off my left wing. I rang the 'bail-out' signal, and I reached out and grabbed the co-pilot out of his seat. I felt the airplane climbing, and I thought to myself, 'If this thing stalls out, and starts falling down backwards, no one is going to get out...'"* —**B-17 pilot**

The Things Our Fathers Saw—The Untold Stories of the World War II Generation-Volume IV: 'Up the Bloody Boot'—The War in Italy

Volume 4 in this series will take you from the deserts of North Africa to the mountains of Italy with the men and women veterans of the Italian campaign who open up about a war that was so brutal, news of it was downplayed at home. The war in the Mediterranean, and particularly the Italian Campaign, is one that for many Americans is shrouded in mystery and murkiness. Yet it was here that the United States launched its first offensive in the west on enemy soil, and it was here that Allied forces would be slogging it out with a tenacious enemy fighting for its life in the longest single American Campaign of World War II.

—*"There was an old French fort there, and we could look down on it during the day. We gauged the way we would hit that place so that the moon would set right between two mountain peaks; we timed it so when we got there, that moon would silhouette them, but not us... We carried out the first and only bayonet charge [of the war] by our Rangers; we didn't fire; very few people knew that we carried out an overnight bayonet attack. I'll tell you, that's something. You see that, it'll shake you up real good." —U.S. Army Ranger, WWII*

— *"We attacked another hill, and I shot a German soldier. And then the Germans counterattacked on the hill, and I could not escape, so I decided to just lay down on top of that soldier and make believe I'm dead. They passed me by, I got up and [this German I shot] starts talking to me in English, he says he's from Coney Island, in Brooklyn; he went to visit his mother in Germany and they put him in the army. And he was dying, and he says to me, 'You can take my cigarettes; you can take my schnapps.' Then he died right underneath me. And I imagine he knew I had shot him....."*
—*U.S. Army scout, WWII*

— *"So there was a terrific fight going on in a place called Santa Ma-ria, south of Rome. While we were going through, in transit, we stopped at a big Italian barn; they had a kitchen set up, and we had our own mess kits. As we were going through the line, we saw this huge rack of shelves with American Army duffel bags packed on there. And Hendrickson said to me, 'Hey, Tony, you know what? My brother must be in the area someplace. There's his duffel bag.' The name was stenciled on. So I said, 'That's nice.' [But] I was thinking, why is his duffel bag there? Well, there was a military policeman guarding these bags. I went back to the MP. I said to him, 'What are these bags doing here?' And I told him about Hendrickson. 'Well,' he said, 'I don't know if you want to tell him, but these guys are all dead. They were all killed at Santa Maria.'"* **—U.S. Army map maker, WWII**

The Things Our Fathers Saw—The Untold Stories of the World War II Generation-Volume V: 'D-Day and Beyond'—The War in France

Volume 5 in this series will take you from the bloody beach at Omaha through the hedgerow country of Normandy and beyond, American veterans of World War II--Army engineers and infantrymen, Coast Guardsmen and Navy sailors, tank gunners and glider pilots--sit down with you across the kitchen table and talk about what they saw and experienced, tales they may have never told anyone before.

— *"I had a vision, if you want to call it that. At my home, the mailman would walk up towards the front porch, and I saw it just as clear as if he's standing beside me—I see his blue jacket and the blue cap and the leather mailbag. Here he goes up to the house, but he doesn't turn. He goes right up the front steps.*

This happened so fast, probably a matter of seconds, but the first thing that came to mind, that's the way my folks would find out what happened to me.

The next thing I know, I kind of come to, and I'm in the push-up mode. I'm half up out of the underwater depression, and I'm trying to figure out what the hell happened to those prone figures on the beach, and all of a sudden, I realized I'm in amongst those bodies!" —Army demolition engineer, Omaha Beach, D-Day

— *"My last mission was the Bastogne mission. We were being towed, we're approaching Bastogne, and I see a cloud of flak, anti-aircraft fire. I said to myself, 'I'm not going to make it.' There were a couple of groups ahead of us, so now the anti-aircraft batteries are zeroing in. Every time a new group came over, they kept zeroing in. My outfit had, I think, 95% casualties." —Glider pilot, D-Day and Beyond*

— *"I was fighting in the hedgerows for five days; it was murder. But psychologically, we were the best troops in the world. There was nobody like us; I had all the training that they could give us, but nothing prepares you for some things.*

You know, in my platoon, the assistant platoon leader got shot right through the head, right through the helmet, dead, right there in front of me. That affects you, doesn't it?" —Paratrooper, D-Day and Beyond

Get it here: matthewrozellbooks.com

ALSO FROM MATTHEW ROZELL

"What healing this has given to the survivors and military men!"-Reviewer

FROM THE <u>ABC WORLD NEWS</u> 'PERSON OF THE WEEK'

A TRAIN NEAR MAGDEBURG

THE HOLOCAUST, AND THE REUNITING

OF THE SURVIVORS AND SOLDIERS, 70 YEARS ON

–Featuring testimony from 15 American liberators and over 30 Holocaust survivors

–73 photographs and illustrations, many never before published; 10 custom maps

–500 pages-extensive notes and bibliographical references

BOOK ONE—THE HOLOCAUST

BOOK TWO—THE AMERICANS

BOOK THREE—LIBERATION

BOOK FOUR—REUNION

Description

THE HOLOCAUST was a watershed event in history. In this book, Matthew Rozell reconstructs a lost chapter—the liberation of a 'death train' deep in the heart of Nazi Germany in the closing days of World War II. Drawing on never-before published eye-witness accounts, survivor testimony, and wartime reports and letters, Rozell brings to life the incredible true stories behind the iconic 1945 liberation photographs taken by the soldiers who were there. He weaves together a chronology of the Holocaust as it unfolds across Europe, and goes back to literally retrace the steps of the survivors and the American soldiers who freed them. Rozell's work results in joyful reunions on three continents, seven decades later. He offers his unique perspective on the lessons of the Holocaust for future generations, and the impact that one person can make.

A selection of comments left by reviewers:

"**Extraordinary research** into an event which needed to be told. I have read many books about the Holocaust and visited various museums but had not heard reference to this train previously. The fact that people involved were able to connect, support and help heal each other emotionally was amazing."

"**The story of the end of the Holocaust and the Nazi regime** told from a very different and precise angle. First-hand accounts from Jewish survivors and the US soldiers that secured their freedom. Gripping."

"**Mr. Rozell travels 'back to the future'** of people who were not promised a tomorrow; neither the prisoners nor the troops knew what horrors the next moment would bring. He captures the parallel experience of soldiers fighting ruthless Nazism and the ruthless treatment of Jewish prisoners."

"**If you have any trepidation** about reading a book on the Holocaust, this review is for you. [Matthew Rozell] masterfully conveys the individual stories of those featured in the book in a manner that does not leave the reader with a sense of despair, but rather a sense of purpose."

"**Could not put this book down**--I just finished reading *A Train Near Magdeburg*. Tears fell as I read pages and I smiled through others. I wish I could articulate the emotions that accompanied me through the stories of these beautiful people."

"**Everyone should read this book,** detailing the amazing bond that formed between Holocaust survivors likely on their way to death in one last concentration camp as WWII was about to end, and a small number of American soldiers that happened upon the stopped train and liberated the victims. The lifelong friendships that resulted between the survivors and their liberators is a testament to compassion and goodness. It is amazing that the author is not Jewish but a "reluctant" history teacher who ultimately becomes a Holocaust scholar. This is a great book."

The original photograph inserted into the official After Action Report. Credit: Major Clarence L. Benjamin. Source: After Action Report, April 1945, 743rd Tank Battalion S-3 Journal History, p. 118.

A photograph taken by an Army major seventy years ago flickers to life on the screen. In it, a profound drama unfolds before the eye. The caption on the museum website reads:

A female survivor and her child run up a hill after escaping from a train near Magdeburg and their liberation by American soldiers from the 743rd Tank Battalion and 30th Infantry Division.

Record Type: Photograph
Date: 1945 April 13
Locale: Farsleben, [Prussian Saxony] Germany
Photographer: Clarence Benjamin
Photo Designation: LIBERATION –
Germany: General
Train to Magdeburg/Farsleben
Keyword:
CHILDREN (0–3 YEARS)
CHILDREN/YOUTH
SURVIVORS
TRAINS
WOMEN

The picture defies expectations. When the terms 'Holocaust' and 'trains' are paired in an online image search, the most common result is that of people being transported to killing centers—but this incredible photograph shows exactly the opposite. And there are many things about this story that will defy expectations. Fifteen years after I brought this haunting image to the light of day, it has been called one of the most powerful photographs of the 20th century. It has been used by museums and memorials across the world, in exhibitions, films, mission appeals, and photo essays. Schoolchildren download it for reports; filmmakers ask to use it in Holocaust documentaries. Yad Vashem, the Israeli Holocaust Martyrs' and Heroes' Remembrance Authority, even employed it as the backdrop for Israel's state ceremonies in the presence of survivors, their president, prime minister, the entire government, top army brass, and the chief rabbi in a national broadcast on the 70th anniversary of the liberation and aftermath of the Holocaust. I know, because they reached out to me for it—me, an ordinary public school teacher, six thousand miles away.

For over half a century, a copy of this photograph and others were hidden away in a shoebox in the back of an old soldier's closet. By spending time with this soldier, I was able to set in motion an extraordinary confluence of events that unfolded organically in the second half of my career as a history teacher. Many of the children who suffered on that train found me, and I was able to link them forever with the men who I had come to know and love, the American GIs who saved them that beautiful April morning. A moment in history is captured on film, and we have reunited the actors, the persecuted, and their liberators, two generations on.

*

It is a cool spring morning. In the background, down the hill, are two cattle cars. If we look closely, we can see a figure sitting on the edge of the opening of a boxcar, perhaps too weak to climb out yet soaking up some energy from the warming April sun. In front of him, a wisp of smoke seems to rise from a small makeshift fire that others have gathered around. The sound of gunfire is echoing nearby; a metallic clanking sound is growing louder at the top of the hill.

This is an appropriate backdrop for the marvel unfolding in the foreground. Now only a few steps away, a woman and perhaps her young daughter are trudging up the hill toward the photographer. The woman has her hair wrapped in a scarf and is clutching the hand of the girl with her right hand. Her left arm is extended outward as if in greeting; her face is turning into a half smile in a mixture of astonishment and enveloping joy, as if she is on the cusp of accepting the belief that she and her daughter have just been saved.

In contrast, the little girl is shooting a sideways glance away from the camera. Her expression is one of distress—she looks terrified.

So what is really happening, and what are the amazing stories behind the picture?

On this morning in Germany in 1945, she may very well be responding to the two Sherman tanks that are now clattering up to the train behind the photographer, who is in the Jeep with the white star.

Following the mother and daughter up the hill towards the soldiers are two other women. One welcomes the tanks with outstretched arms and a wide grin as she moves up the hill. The other follows behind her. She appears to be crying.

It is Friday, the 13th of April, 1945. Led by their major scouting in a Jeep, Tanks 12 and 13 of 'D' Company, 743rd Tank Battalion, US Army, have just liberated a train transport with thousands of sick and emaciated victims of the Holocaust. In an instant, Major Clarence L. Benjamin snaps a photograph so fresh and raw that if one did not know better, one might think it was from a modern cellphone, although it will be soon buried into his official report back to headquarters.

But what have they stumbled upon? Where have these people come from?

And what do the soldiers do now?

*

In this book, you will learn of the tragedies and the triumphs behind the photograph. You will enter the abyss of the Holocaust with me, which the United States Holocaust Memorial Museum defines as 'the systematic, bureaucratic, state-sponsored persecution and murder of six million Jews by the Nazi regime and its collaborators.' You will meet the survivors of that train as they immerse you in their worlds as civilization collapsed around them. We will visit the camps and authentic sites together, and we will trace the route of the brave Americans who found themselves confronted with industrial-scale genocide. And I will lead you safely out of the chasm as we witness the aftermath, the miracles of liberation and reunification, seven decades later.

In many respects, this story should still be buried, because there is no logical way to explain my role in the climactic aftermath. I was born sixteen years after the killing stopped, a continent away from the horrors and comfortably unaware of the events of the Holocaust and World War II for much of my life. I was raised in the sanctuary of a nurturing community and an intact family. I am not Jewish and had never even been inside a synagogue until my forties. I'm not observantly religious, but I am convinced that I was chosen to affirm and attest to what I have experienced. In this book I rewind the tape to reconstruct how indeed it all came to be—the horrors of the experiences of the Holocaust survivors, the ordeals and sacrifices of the American soldiers, and the miracles of liberation and reunification.

As the curtain descends on a career spanning four decades, consider this also one teacher's testament—a memoir of sorts, but more a story of being caught up as an integral part of something much bigger than myself, driven by some invisible force which has conquered the barriers of time and space. I too became a witness, and this is what I saw.

Matthew Rozell

Visit my shop at matthewrozellbooks.com for more.

ABOUT THE AUTHOR

Photo Credit: Joan K. Lentini; May, 2017.

Matthew Rozell is an award-winning history teacher, author, speaker, and blogger on the topic of the most cataclysmic events in the history of mankind—World War II and the Holocaust. Rozell has been featured as the 'ABC World News Person of the Week' and has had his work as a teacher filmed for the CBS Evening News, NBC Learn, the Israeli Broadcast Authority, the United States Holocaust Memorial Museum, and the New York State United Teachers. He writes on the power of teaching and the importance of the study of history at TeachingHistoryMatters.com, and you can 'Like' his Facebook author page at MatthewRozellBooks for updates.

Mr. Rozell is a sought-after speaker on World War II, the Holocaust, and history education, motivating and inspiring his audiences with the lessons of the past. Visit MatthewRozell.com for availability/details.

About this Book/

Acknowledgements

*

A note on historiographical style and convention: to enhance accuracy, consistency, and readability, I corrected punctuation and spelling and sometimes even place names, but only after extensive research. I did take the liberty of occasionally condensing the speaker's voice, eliminating side tangents or incidental information not relevant to the matter at hand. Sometimes two or more interviews with the same person were combined for readability and narrative flow. All of the words of the subjects, however, are essentially their own.

Additionally, I chose to utilize footnotes and endnotes where I deemed them appropriate, directing readers who wish to learn more to my sources, notes, and side commentary. I hope that they do not detract from the flow of the narrative.

*

First, I will always acknowledge the hundreds of students who passed through my classes and who forged the bonds with the World War II generation. I promised you this book someday, and now that many of you are yourselves parents, you can tell your children this book is for them. Who says young people are indifferent to the past? Here is evidence to the contrary.

The Hudson Falls Central School District and my former colleagues have my deep appreciation for supporting this endeavor and recognizing its significance throughout the years.

For helpful feedback and suggestions on the original manuscript I am indebted to my good friend and trusted critic, Alan Bush. Alan always offers solid advice, diving into the narrative as soon as it arrives in his inbox, saving me perhaps a good deal of anguish with his timely and trusted comments. Additionally, Sunny Buchman was one of my early champions and worked to arrange interviews with the folks at her retirement community, The Glen at Hiland Meadows. My wife Laura re-typed some of the seventy-five-year-old letters and reports. My friend Rob Miller traveled to my hometown to take some very special portraits of our veterans and participate in some of our events recognizing them. The Folklife Center at Crandall Public Library in Glens Falls helped with background information on the *LOOK Magazine* series that profiled the Glens Falls–North Country region as 'Hometown, USA' during the war. To my good friend and classmate Paul Dietrich, thanks for finally getting me on board to experience firsthand a deafening, lumbering B-17 flight up Lake George and back.

Naturally this work would not have been possible had it not been for the willingness of the veterans to share their stories for posterity. Andy Doty graciously allowed me to use excerpts from his well-written war autobiography. All of the veterans who were interviewed for this book had the foresight to complete release forms granting access to their stories, and for us to share the information with the New York State Military Museum's Veterans Oral History Project, where copies of most of the interviews reside. Wayne Clarke and Mike Russert of the NYSMMVOP were instrumental in cultivating this relationship with my classes over the years, and are responsible for some of the interviews in this book as well. Please see the 'Source Notes.'

I would be remiss if I did not recall the profound influence of my late mother and father, Mary and Tony Rozell, both cutting edge educators and proud early supporters of my career. To my younger siblings Mary, Ned, Nora, and Drew, all accomplished writers and authors, thank you for your encouragement as well. Final and deepest appreciations go to my wife Laura and our children, Emma, Ned, and Mary. Thank you for indulging the old man as he attempted to bring to life the stories he collected as a young one.

NOTES

[1] Bailey, Ronald H. *The Air War in Europe.* Alexandria, Virginia: Time-Life Books, 1979. 28.

[2] Bailey, Ronald H. *The Air War in Europe.* Alexandria, Virginia: Time-Life Books, 1979. 29.

[3] Bailey, Ronald H. *The Air War in Europe.* Alexandria, Virginia: Time-Life Books, 1979. 30.

[4] Miller, Donald L. *The Story of World War II.* New York: Simon & Schuster, 2001. 38

[5] Bailey, Ronald H. *The Air War in Europe.* Alexandria, Virginia: Time-Life Books, 1979. 28.

[6] Tooze, Adam. *The Wages of Destruction: The Making and Breaking of the Nazi Economy.* London: Allen Lane, 2007. Location 7803

[7] Miller, Donald L. *The Story of World War II.* New York: Simon & Schuster, 2001. 257.

[8] *45,000 people were killed and 400,000 left homeless* -Miller, Donald L. *The Story of World War II.* New York: Simon & Schuster, 2001. 259.

[9] 'B-17 Flying Fortress', Boeing http://www.boeing.com/history/products/b-17-flying-fortress.page

[10] Ambrose, Steven. *The Wild Blue: The Men and the Boys Who Flew the B-24s over Germany.* New York: Simon & Schuster, 2001. 23

[11] Miller, Donald L., *The Story of World War II.* New York: Simon & Schuster, 2001. 483.

[12] For an excellent discussion of the Tuskegee Airmen, see the CAF Red Tail Squadron website, http://www.redtail.org. "The CAF Red Tail Squadron is a volunteer-driven organization dedicated to educating audiences across the country about the history

and legacy of the Tuskegee Airmen, America's first black military pilots and their support personnel."

[13] CAF Red Tail Squadron website, www.redtail.org.

[14] CAF Red Tail Squadron website, www.redtail.org.

[15] Imperial War Museum, Richard J Faulkner. www.americanairmuseum.com/person/182944

[16] Miller, Donald L., *The Story of World War II*. New York: Simon & Schuster, 2001. 217.

[17] Miller, Donald L. *Masters of the Air: America's Bomber Boys Who Fought the Air War against Nazi Germany*. New York: Simon & Schuster, 2006. 493.

[18] Nichol, John, and Rennell, Tony. *The Last Escape: The Untold Story of Allied Prisoners of War in Germany 1944-1945*. London: Viking, 2002.

[19] Miller, 495.

[20] Miller, 496.

[21] Source Notes: **Clarence W Dart.** Interviewed by Matthew Rozell, December 2003.

[22] Source Notes: **John G. Weeks.** Interviewed by Michael Russert and Wayne Clarke, May 22, 2002. Deposited at NYS Military Museum. Also, John G. Weeks' unpublished memoir, 'The Story of a Photo Reconnaissance Pilot during World War II.'

[23] Source Notes: **Richard Faulkner.** Interviewed by Michael Russert and Wayne Clarke, September 24, 2003. Auburn, NY. Deposited at NYS Military Museum.

[24] Source Notes: **George FitzGibbon.** Interviewed by Michael Russert and Wayne Clarke, May 18, 2002. Johnson City, NY. Deposited at NYS Military Museum.

[25] Source Notes: **Charles Corea.** Interviewed by Michael Aikey and Wayne Clarke, November 20, 2001. Rochester, New York. Deposited at NYS Military Museum.

[26] Source Notes: **Earl M. Morrow, Sam Lisica, Jerry Silverman.** Interviewed by Matthew Rozell, July 31, 2001. Hartford, NY. Deposited at NYS Military Museum.